CHERRY CREATIONS

CHERRY CREATIONS

The Ultimate Cherry Cookbook

Dr. Myles H. Bader

Northstar Publishing Co.
Las Vegas, Nevada

Additional copies of this book may be ordered through
bookstores or by sending $15.95 plus $3.50 for
postage and handling to:

 Northstar Publishing Co.
1818 Industrial Dr. Suite 209
Las Vegas, NV   89102
800-717-6001

 PUBLISHERS DESIGN SERVICE
PROJECT COORDINATORS: ALEX MOORE/ERIN LEACH
COVER DESIGN: DEBRA ANTON
TEXT DESIGN: DEBRA ANTON
ILLUSTRATIONS: MARY BLUE

1 3 5 7 9 10 8 6 4 2

Publisher's Cataloging-in-Publication Data
Bader, Myles H.
Cherry creations: the ultimate cherry cookbook/
Myles H. Bader – Las Vegas, NV:
Northstar Pub., c1995.

p.   ill.   cm.

1. Cookery (Cherries) I. Title.
TX813.c4B33   1995
641.6'423-dc20   94-77704

Printed in the United States of America

ISBN 0-9646741-1-4

DEDICATION

This cookbook is dedicated to the cherry growers of the United States. Without these families and their hard work, there would be no product. We commend them for their commitment towards providing a product that brings smiles and pleasure to millions of people around the world each year.

CONTENTS

FOREWORD

Cherry Creations, The Ultimate Cherry Cookbook
contains many delicious recipes using cherries. It is the
result of cooperation from many facets of the cherry
industry, including chefs, farm-based cooks and others.
The National Cherry Festival, an acclaimed
family attraction, celebrates the cherry annually.

Much of what you'll find in this cookbook is the result of a
continual search by The National Cherry Festival for
outstanding recipes. Every year, this organization hosts a
recipe search and contest for amateur chefs to cook up what
they believe to be unique gourmet cherry fare.
The "Taste of Cherries" event, presented by the Chicago
Tribune and Mountain Jack's Restaurants, and directed by
Penny Lautner, collects up to 100 recipes from
throughout the Midwest. In cooperation with its sponsors,
the National Cherry Festival's "Taste of Cherries" produces a
scholarship for students pursuing a career in the culinary arts field.

*Additionally, **Cherry Creations, The Ultimate Cherry***
***Cookbook** has drawn special "Chef's Secrets" and facts*
from Michigan cherry producers and farm families who grow,
harvest, and process 75% of the United States tart cherries -
primarily in the Grand Traverse area of Northwest
Michigan, which is the Cherry Capital of the World.

Special appreciation goes to the many chefs and industry
leaders who have taken the cherry in many
new directions, including Ray Pleva. Pleva, who has
combined his knack of meat processing and cherry growing
to produce Plevalean® (ground beef with cherries)

*and Cherry Pecan Sausage, began "taste testing" at
the National Cherry Festival over twenty-five years ago.*

*This cookbook will lead you to hundreds of
tantalizing recipes, all utilizing the prized
fruit - the cherry! Kudos to all those who have
made this book possible.*

Susan Wilcox Olson
Media Relations

Chuck O'Connor
Director of Marketing

National Cherry Festival

PREFACE

Cherries are one of the most versatile of all fruits. They are juicy, sweet and colorful and can be easily used for hundreds of recipes with excellent results. A cup of cherries contains only 110 calories and has an abundance of nutrients.

Cherries are a close relative of the plum family and a distant relative of the peach and nectarine family. They are grown in only 20 countries worldwide of which the United States is the leading producer. Seventy percent of all cherries grown in the U.S. are grown in Michigan, Washington, Oregon, Idaho, Utah and California.

The cherry recipes found in this book have been gathered from award winning recipes and executive chefs from all corners of the world. In Europe a popular cherry dish is chilled cherry soup, and in many countries cherries are only used for special occasion garnishments.

Freezing fresh cherries is a common practice to extend their period of availability. Cherries will freeze well for up to a year.

ACKNOWLEDGEMENTS

*Without the help of many people, this book would
not be possible. I would especially like to thank:
Jerrold Jenkins, Mark Dressler, Erin Leach,
Gabrielle Shaw, Laura Pratt and
Alex Moore of Publishers Design Service;
Debra Anton and Mary Blue of Debra Anton Design Studio;
and Chuck O'Connor of the National Cherry Festival.*

	TART CHERRIES	SWEET CHERRIES
MOST COMMON FORMS	Canned Frozen Dried Note: Tart cherries are seldom sold fresh, because they are highly perishable.	Fresh Note: Sweet cherries are also commercially canned and frozen. And, some are processed into maraschino cherries.
MAJOR USAGE	Desserts Main courses Side dishes or salads Breads	Snacking, one by one

FLAVOR AND APPEARANCE	Montmorency
	  Tangy flavor
	  Bright red color
		Bing and Lambert
		  Sweet, rich flavor
		  Dark red/mahogany color
		  Large, plump, firm
		Rainier
		  Mild, very sweet
		  Golden with red blush
		  Extra large, fine-textured

SUMMER SNACK IDEAS	Top sundaes or ice cream pies with cherry filling and topping. Tuck packages of dried cherries into knapsacks for camping or hiking. Stir tart cherries into yogurt or pudding. Puree cherry filling for a quick barbecue sauce that's great with ribs or chicken.	Fresh out of hand bite-size refreshment, one by one. Serve with other fresh fruits or use as a garnish. Add to ice cream or frozen yogurt. Freeze and use as a refreshing snack or as tasty ice cubes to cool your summer drinks.
SEASON	July harvest Because most tart cherries are canned, frozen or dried, they are available year round.	May to mid-August

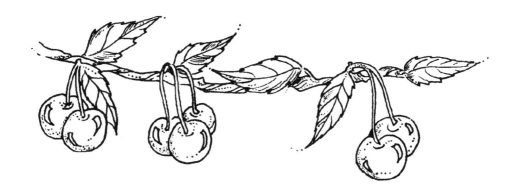

CHERRY VARIETIES

TART

MONTMORENCY - Usually round but slightly compressed. Very juicy and a clear medium-red color. Excellent for pies, tarts and jams. This is the most widely grown tart cherry in the United States.

EARLY RICHMOND - Round; medium-red color with tender flesh and a tough, thin skin. Not generally grown in the United States.

ENGLISH MORELLO - A round shaped cherry, very deep red in color becoming almost black. The flesh is red, tender, and somewhat tart. It is not grown commercially in large quantities in the United States.

SWEET

REPUBLICAN - (Also called Lewellan) It is small to medium-sized, heart-shaped with crisp flesh ranging from very red to purplish-black. The juice is very dark and sweet.

ROYAL ANN - (Also called Napoleon and Emperor Francis) These are heart-shaped and light golden in color. The flesh may be pink to light red; usually firm and juicy with an excellent flavor. The light flesh variety is used commercially in canning.

BING – These are usually very large, heart-shaped with flesh that ranges in color from deep red to almost black. The skin is usually smooth and glossy.

SCHMIDT – Similar to the Bing Cherry.

TARTARIAN – Very large, heart-shaped with purplish to black flesh. Very tender and sweet. The skin is thin and one of the most popular cherries of the mid-season.

CHAPMAN - Large round, purplish-black flesh. Produced from a seedling of the Black Tartarian variety. The fruit usually matures early in the season.

LAMBERT – A very large, usually round cherry with a dark to very dark red flesh. Very firm and meaty.

CHERRY
CREATIONS

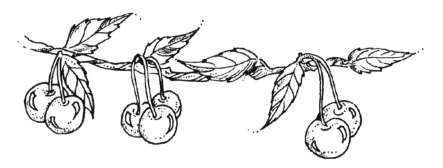

APPETIZERS

Spicy Cherry Meatballs

Cherry Mushroom Appetizers

Cold Hungarian Cherry Soup

Carrots with Character

Cherry Chedder Toasts

Sensational Stuffed Mushrooms

Cherry Crab Spread

The list goes on and on of more
Awesome Appetizers...

SPICY CHERRY MEATBALLS

1 1/2 pounds Plevalean® (91% lean ground beef with cherries)
1 cup fine bread crumbs
1 tablespoon parsley flakes
3/4 teaspoon salt
1/2 teaspoon basil
1/4 teaspoon black pepper
1/4 teaspoon garlic powder
2 teaspoons Worcestershire sauce
dash of red pepper
1 tablespoon minced dry onion
1/4 cup dry milk powder
1/3 cup catsup

Combine above ingredients and mix thoroughly. Shape into one inch balls. Place in a single layer on a greased baking pan at 400 degrees for 12 minutes. Remove from pan and put in a large baking casserole. Lower oven temperature to 350 degrees. Make cherry sauce and pour over meatballs. Bake in a covered casserole for 45 minutes. Stir meatballs twice during baking time.

SPICY CHERRY MEATBALL SAUCE

2 cups tart red cherries (1 quart fresh) or 1 can (16 ounces) pitted tart cherries (drained)
2/3 cup cherry preserves
1 cup (12 ounce bottle) seafood cocktail sauce
2 cans (15 ounce) tomato sauce
2 tablespoons horseradish
2 tablespoons Dijon mustard

Mix all ingredients in a medium saucepan. Cook over medium heat for five minutes. Pour over meatballs. Makes enough sauce for four dozen meatballs.

Plevalean® makes a very lean meatball. The cherries in the sauce and meat make a very tender and tasty meatball. You will notice a delicious flavor without the fat.

Cherries originated in Asia Minor and were named for a Turkish town Cerasus, which is presently called Giresun, located on the Black Sea.

CHERRY-MUSHROOM APPETIZERS

30 large mushrooms (about 1 pound)
1/2 pound bulk pork sausage
1 cup dried cherries, chopped (see note)
2 green onions, sliced
1 package (8 ounces) cream cheese, softened

Pull stems from mushrooms and discard (or save for another use). Rinse mushroom caps; drain well. Set aside.

Break sausage into small pieces and put in a microwave-safe dish. Microwave, uncovered, on HIGH (100% power) 1 minute. Stir with a wooden spoon to break sausage into small pieces. Microwave on HIGH 1 to 2 minutes longer, or until sausage is cooked. Add chopped dried cherries and sliced onions to sausage; mix well. Add cream cheese and stir until all ingredients are well blended. Fill each mushroom cap with a heaping spoonful of sausage mixture. Place filled mushrooms in a microwave-safe pie plate or other round container. Microwave about 12 mushrooms at a time on HIGH 3 to 4 minutes (rotating dish once), or until mushrooms and filling are hot. Serve immediately. Makes 30.

Note: Dried cherries are available at gourmet and specialty food stores.

TANGY CHERRY MEATBALLS

2 pounds extra lean ground beef
1 cup cornflake crumbs
1/3 cup dried parsley flakes
1/3 cup ketchup
2 eggs
2 tablespoons soy sauce
2 tablespoons instant minced onion
1/2 teaspoon garlic powder
1/4 teaspoon ground black pepper
1 can (21 ounces) cherry filling and topping
1 bottle (12 ounces) chili sauce
2 tablespoons firmly packed sugar
1 tablespoon lemon juice

In a large mixing bowl, combine beef, cornflake crumbs, parsley flakes, ketchup, eggs, soy sauce, minced onion, garlic powder and pepper. Mix well. Shape into 1 inch balls; place in a 13 x 9 x 2 inch baking pan. In a medium saucepan, combine cherry filling, chili sauce, brown sugar and lemon juice. Mix well. Cook over medium heat, stirring occasionally, 5 to 10 minutes, or until sauce is hot. Pour sauce over meatballs. Bake, uncovered, in a preheated 350 degree oven 30 minutes. Makes 40 to 60 meatballs.

COLD HUNGARIAN CHERRY SOUP

4 cups fresh tart cherries, pitted (see note)
3 cups water plus 3 tablespoons water, divided
1 cup granulated sugar
1 stick cinnamon
2 tablespoons all-purpose flour
1 cup heavy cream
1 cup red wine

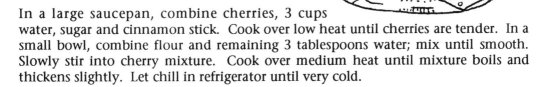

In a large saucepan, combine cherries, 3 cups water, sugar and cinnamon stick. Cook over low heat until cherries are tender. In a small bowl, combine flour and remaining 3 tablespoons water; mix until smooth. Slowly stir into cherry mixture. Cook over medium heat until mixture boils and thickens slightly. Let chill in refrigerator until very cold.

Makes 6 servings.

Note: 2 cans (16 ounces each) pitted, tart cherries can be used, if fresh tart cherries are not available. Use the liquid from the cans to replace part of the water.

CHERRY CHEDDAR TOASTS

French bread
Butter or margarine
Canned sweet cherries, chopped and well-drained
Shredded Cheddar cheese

Slice bread on the diagonal into 1/2 inch slices. Spread each slice with small amount of butter. Place buttered bread on a cookie sheet. Bake in a preheated 375 degree oven 10 minutes, or until lightly browned. Remove toast from oven, but leave on cookie sheet. Put 1 teaspoon chopped cherries on each piece of toast; cover with cheese. Broil 4 to 5 inches from the heat just until the cheese melts. Serve immediately as an appetizer or snack.

Makes as many as you want.

Fun Cherry Facts...

It is believed that birds brought the cherries to Europe and early settlers brought them to America.

In 1629 the first production cherry was the Red Kentish variety in Massachusetts.

CHERRY BRUSCHETTA

An appetite teaser or light lunch.

1 can (21 ounces) cherry filling and topping
1/2 cup finely chopped red onion
1/2 teaspoon dried basil
1/2 teaspoon dried oregano
2 garlic cloves, minced
1/4 cup olive oil
1 loaf (16 ounces) French bread, cut into 3/4 inch slices.

In a medium saucepan, combine cherry filling, onion, basil and oregano; mix well. Cook, stirring constantly, over medium heat 5 minutes, or until mixture is bubbly and flavors are blended. Let cool to room temperature. In a small bowl, combine garlic and olive oil. Brush both sides of each bread slice with oil mixture; place on an ungreased baking sheet. Broil, 4 to 5 inches from the heat, 1 to 2 minutes per side, or until golden brown. Top each slice of bread with a generous tablespoon of cherry mixture. Serve immediately as an appetizer or first course.

Makes 8 servings.

Serving size: 2 slices of bread, 321 calories per serving. Total fat per serving: 5.5 grams.

PORK AND DRIED CHERRY EMPAÑADILLAS

An appetizer or light dinner, these meaty morsels will be a hit with family and guests.

1/2 cup chopped dried tart cherries
1/4 cup sherry cooking wine
3/4 pound bulk pork sausage
1 teaspoon ground cumin
1/4 teaspoon ground ginger
1/8 teaspoon cayenne pepper
1/4 cup chopped pine nuts
1/4 cup chopped green onions
4 (9 inch) refrigerated pie crusts
1 egg, beaten with 1 teaspoon water

In a small saucepan over medium heat, warm cherries and sherry about 3 minutes. Remove from heat. Let stand, covered 10 minutes. Meanwhile, in a skillet over medium heat, cook sausage 5 to 6 minutes, or until browned. Pour off fat. Add cumin, ginger, cayenne, cherry mixture, pine nuts and green onions; mix well. Set aside.

Roll each pie crust into a 9 x 12 inch rectangle; cut each crust into 12 (3 inch) squares. Place 1 heaping teaspoon pork and cherry filling in center of each square. Fold over one corner to form a triangle. Seal by brushing edges lightly with water and crimping with a fork. Place on ungreased baking sheets; brush with egg wash. Bake in a preheated 400 degree oven 12 to 15 minutes, or until lightly brown.

Empañar, a Spanish word, means "to bake in pastry". Empañadillas are single-serving, pastry crust turnovers, filled with a savory meat mixture.

Makes 48 empañadillas

Serving size: 2 empañadillas, 226 calories per serving. Total fat per serving: 16 grams

BRIE TORTE

Well-wrapped, this appetizer will keep in the refrigerator for at least two weeks.

1 wedge (about 8 ounces) Brie cheese
1/4 cup butter or margarine, softened
1/4 cup chopped dried tart cherries
3 tablespoons finely chopped pecans
1/2 teaspoon dried thyme

Refrigerate Brie until chilled and firm; or freeze 30 minutes until firm. Cut wedge in half horizontally.

In a small bowl, combine butter, cherries, pecans and thyme; mix well. Evenly spread mixture on cut-side of one of the Brie wedges. Top with other half, cut-side down. Lightly press together. Wrap in plastic wrap; refrigerate 1 to 2 hours. To serve, bring cheese to room temperature. Serve with plain crackers.

Makes 10 servings.

Serving size: 2 tablespoons, 139 calories per serving. Total fat per serving: 12 grams.

More Fun Cherry Facts...

The United States consumes approximately 150,000 tons of cherries annually.

50% of the sweet cherries and 90% of the sour cherries are canned or frozen.

Cherries were brought to Rome by Lucullus, who loved food and luxury.

CHERRY CRAB SPREAD

Crabmeat impresses guests and cherries provide pizzazz.

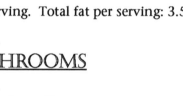

1 package (8 ounces) Lite-cream cheese, softened
2 tablespoons 1% milk
1 can (7 ounces) crabmeat, drained and flaked
1 tablespoon chopped green onion
1/4 teaspoon seasoned salt
1/8 teaspoon garlic powder
1/2 cup chopped dried tart cherries
Chopped fresh parsley or sliced green onions, for garnish (optional)

In a small bowl, beat cream cheese and milk until fluffy. Add crabmeat, green onions, seasoned salt and garlic powder; mix well. Stir in cherries. Let chill. Garnish with parsley or green onions, if desired. Serve with crackers.

Makes about 2 cups.

Serving size: 2 tablespoons, 73 calories per serving. Total fat per serving: 3.5 grams.

SENSATIONAL STUFFED MUSHROOMS

Hot out of the oven, mushrooms are an elegant appetizer.

30 large mushrooms (about 1 pound)
1/2 pound bulk pork sausage
1 cup chopped dried tart cherries
2 green onion, sliced
1 package (8 ounce) Lite-cream cheese, softened

Pull stems from mushrooms and discard (or save for another use). Rinse mushroom caps; drain will. Set aside. In a large skillet, cook sausage, stirring to break up meat, 5 minutes, or until sausage is done. Remove from heat. Add dried cherries, onions and cream cheese; mix well. Fill each mushroom cap with a heaping teaspoonful of sausage mixture. Place filled mushrooms on a lightly greased baking sheet. Bake in a preheated 425 degree oven 6 to 8 minutes. Serve immediately.

Makes 30

Serving size: 2 mushrooms, 148 calories per serving. Total fat per serving: 10 grams.

Fresh mushrooms should be wiped with a damp paper towel or rinsed briefly in cold water and dried thoroughly. Mushrooms should never be soaked because they absorb water and become mushy.

CARROTS WITH CHARACTER

Plain carrots become elegant with cherries, nutmeg and ginger.

1 pound carrots, peeled and sliced
1 cup frozen unsweetened tart cherries
3 tablespoons maple syrup
2 tablespoons butter or margarine
1/2 teaspoon ground nutmeg
1/4 teaspoon ground ginger

In a medium saucepan, cook carrots in water, covered, 8 - 10 minutes, or until tender. Drain well. In a greased 1 1/2 quart baking dish, combine cooked carrots, cherries, maple syrup, butter, nutmeg and ginger. (It is not necessary to thaw cherries before combining with carrots.) Bake, uncovered, in a preheated 375 degree oven 35 minutes, or until hot and bubbly. Stir occasionally.

Makes 6 servings. Serving size: 1/2 cup, 105 calories per serving.

SPICED CHERRY-HAM HORS D'OEUVRES

1/2 cup canned or frozen tart cherries
2 tablespoons sugar
2 1/4 teaspoons cornstarch
1/8 teaspoon ground cloves
1/8 teaspoon allspice
1 or 2 drops red food coloring
1 package 10 count refrigerator biscuits
3 ounces Lite-cream cheese, room temperature
1 tablespoon 2 % milk
3 ounces thinly sliced ham

Drain cherries, reserving liquid. Chop cherries. Mix sugar, cornstarch, cloves and allspice in saucepan. Stir in the liquid from the cherries plus enough water to make 1 cup liquid. Bring to a boil, stirring constantly. Reduce heat and cook 5 minutes. Remove from heat. Stir in cherries and food coloring.

Cut biscuits in half. Flatten each piece into a 2 inch circle on a lightly greased cookie sheet. For soft sides, put biscuits almost touching; for crunchier sides, put biscuits 1 inch apart. Mix cream cheese and milk; spread mixture thinly on circles. Arrange bits of ham over cheese Top each with a heaping teaspoon of cherry mixture. Bake at 450 degrees for 8 minutes. Serve warm.

Makes 20.

SALADS

Endive Salad with Cherries,
Roquefort and Walnuts

Black Sweet Cherry Salad
with a Zip

Festive Cherry Salad

Pretty in Pink Salad

Unbelievable and Amazing

Combinations for Salads...

CHERRY SALAD SUPREME

1 package (3 ounces) raspberry-flavored gelatin
1 can (21 ounces) cherry filling and topping
1 package (3 ounces) lemon-flavored gelatin
1 package (3 ounces) cream cheese, softened
1/3 cup mayonnaise
1 can (8 3/4 ounces) crushed pineapple
1/2 cup heavy cream
1 cup miniature marshmallows
2 tablespoons chopped walnuts

In a large mixing bowl, combine raspberry-flavored gelatin and 1 cup boiling water; mix until gelatin is dissolved. Stir in cherry filling; mix well. Pour gelatin mixture into a 9 x 9 x 2 inch or 11 x 7 x 2 inch baking dish; let chill until partially set. In another mixing bowl, combine lemon-flavored gelatin and 1 cup boiling water; mix until gelatin is dissolved. In a small bowl combine cream cheese and mayonnaise; stir cream cheese mixture into lemon-flavored gelatin; beat until smooth. Add undrained pineapple; mix well. In a small mixing bowl with an electric mixer, beat heavy cream until stiff. Gently fold whipped cream and marshmallows into lemon-flavored gelatin mixture. Spread on top of chilled cherry layer; top with walnuts. Let chill until both gelatin layers are set.

Makes 8 to 12 servings.

CHERRY TRAIL MIX SALAD

1 bunch (about 1 pound) broccoli
1/2 pound bacon
1/2 cup chopped onion
1 cup dried cherries
3/4 cup (6 ounces) shelled sunflower seeds
1 1/2 cups shredded Colby or Monterey Jack cheese
1/2 cup mayonnaise
1/2 cup non-fat yogurt
2 tablespoons cherry or raspberry vinaigrette dressing

Rinse broccoli and cut into bite-size pieces. In a skillet or microwave oven, cook bacon until crisp. Drain well and break into small pieces. In a large mixing bowl, combine broccoli, bacon, onion, cherries, sunflower seeds and cheese; mix well. In a small container, combine mayonnaise, yogurt and vinaigrette dressing; mix well. Pour over broccoli mixture to coat all ingredients. Refrigerate until ready to serve.

Makes 6 servings.

ENDIVE SALAD WITH CHERRIES, ROQUEFORT AND WALNUTS

1 small head endive, rinsed and drained
1 small head butter lettuce, rinsed and drained
3/4 cup walnut oil
3 tablespoons sherry wine vinegar
1 tablespoons lemon juice
Salt and pepper, to taste
1/2 cup fresh sweet cherries, rinsed and pitted
1/2 cup walnuts, toasted
4 ounces Roquefort cheese, crumbled
2 tablespoons minced chives

Tear endive and lettuce into bite-sized pieces and put in a large salad bowl. In a small container, combine walnut oil, vinegar and lemon juice; beat with a wire whisk until well-blended. Season dressing with salt and pepper. Drizzle dressing over endive and lettuce; mix well to coat all with dressing. Arrange lettuce and endive on salad plates. Top each serving with a portion of cherries, toasted walnuts, Roquefort cheese and chives.

Makes 4 to 6 servings.

Note: This salad tastes best when the dressing is made in advance and chilled thoroughly before adding to endive and lettuce.

BLACK SWEET CHERRY SALAD WITH A ZIP

2 cans (16 ounces each) black sweet cherries
1 can (8 ounces) crushed pineapple
1/4 cup black cherry schnapps
1/2 cup granulated sugar
1 package (6 ounces) cherry-flavored gelatin
1 cup lemon juice
1/2 cup orange juice

Drain cherries and pineapple reserving juices. Put cherries in a small bowl with black cherry schnapps. Marinate 15 minutes, then drain cherries, reserving the schnapps. Combine reserved juice from cherries and pineapple and reserved schnapps to make 2 cups; discard any leftover liquid. Put the juice-schnapps mixture into a saucepan; bring to a boil. Remove from heat. Add sugar and gelatin; stir until dissolved. Stir in drained cherries and pineapple, walnuts, orange juice and lemon juice; mix well. Pour into a 9 x 13 x 2 inch pan. Let chill until firm.

Makes 10 to 12 servings.

> ## How About These Tips...
>
> *Try brushing the bottom crust of cherry pies with egg whites to prevent the fruit juices from soaking in.*
>
> *To keep a cherry cake from drying out, attach slices of bread with tooth picks to any exposed cut edges of the cake.*

DRIED CHERRY SPINACH SALAD

This salad is also lowfat and low-calorie.

1/2 cup olive oil
1/2 cup granulated sugar
2 1/2 tablespoons vinegar or lemon juice
5 tablespoons chili sauce
Dash black pepper
2 hard-cooked eggs, peeled and chopped
4 to 6 slices bacon, fried and crumbled
1/2 pound fresh mushrooms, sliced
1/2 cup sliced water chestnuts
1/2 cup dried tart cherries
10 ounces fresh spinach, stems removed,
rinsed and drained

In a jar with a lid, combine oil, sugar, vinegar, chili sauce and pepper. Cover and shake well. Refrigerate, covered, at least 1 hour to let flavors blend.

Just before serving, combine spinach, eggs, bacon, mushrooms, water chestnuts and cherries in a large serving bowl; toss well. Shake salad dressing well before mixing into spinach mixture.

Makes 6 servings.

CHERRY AMBROSIA

This salad is lowfat and low in calories.

1 large bunch red leaf lettuce (or lettuce of your choice)
1 package (4.5 ounce) Michigan dried cherries
1 can (16 ounce) dark sweet cherries, well-drained
2 large navel oranges, peeled
1 large bunch green seedless grapes
1 (8 ounces) lowfat vanilla yogurt
1 ounce slivered almonds

Arrange lettuce on large serving platter. Arrange 10 orange sections on top of lettuce. Set aside. In large bowl, combine remaining orange sections (cut up), dried cherries, dark sweet cherries, grapes, yogurt and almonds (reserve a few for garnish). Toss lightly. Just before serving, place cherry mixture in center of lettuce. Garnish with remaining almonds.

Serves 6 - 8.

FESTIVE CHERRY SALAD

This is a lowfat salad.

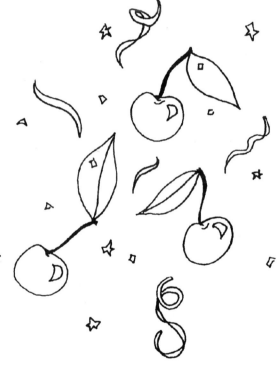

DRESSING:
1/4 cup canola oil
2 tablespoons cherry vinegar
1 tablespoon snipped parsley
2 tablespoons sugar
1/2 teaspoon salt/dash pepper
dash tabasco sauce

Shake ingredients in tightly covered jar and then refrigerate.

SALAD:
1/4 cup almonds
1 tablespoon plus 1 teaspoon sugar
1 large head Romaine lettuce or
combination of lettuce types
2 large stalks celery, diced
4 green onions, diced
1/2 - 1 quart pitted fresh cherries.

Cook almonds and sugar over medium heat, stirring constantly until sugar has melted. Cool. Wash and dry lettuce. Refrigerate to allow crispness. Add remaining ingredients just before serving. Add dressing and toss.

CHERRY-CRAN SALAD

1 can (16 ounces) pitted, tart cherries
1 package (3 ounces) cherry-flavored gelatin
1 can (8 ounces) cranberry sauce
1 package (3 ounces) lemon-flavored gelatin
1 package (3 ounces) cream cheese, softened or whipped topping

Drain cherries, reserving liquid from can. Add enough water to the liquid to make 1 cup. In a large saucepan, bring the liquid to a boil. Remove from heat. Stir in cherry-flavored gelatin; mix until gelatin is dissolved. Add cranberry sauce, breaking it up with a fork and stirring until smooth. Stir in cherries. Pour gelatin into a 9 x 9 x 2 inch pan; let chill until almost set.

In a mixing bowl, dissolve lemon flavored gelatin in 1 cup boiling water. In a small bowl, combine cream cheese and mayonnaise; beat until smooth. Gradually add cream cheese mixture to lemon gelatin. Stir in undrained pineapple. Let lemon gelatin mixture chill until partly set, then fold in whipped cream. Spread lemon gelatin mixture over cherry gelatin layer. Cover and let chill until firm.

Makes 8 to 10 servings.

CHERRY COLA SALAD

1 can (16 ounces) pitted, dark sweet cherries
1 can (15 ounces) crushed pineapple, reserving juices.

Add enough water to the juices to make 2 cups liquid. Put liquid in a saucepan and bring to a boil.

In a large mixing bowl, combine cherry flavored gelatin and boiling liquid. Stir to dissolve gelatin. Add cream cheese to hot gelatin; stir until cream cheese melts. Stir in cola flavored carbonated beverage, cherries, pineapple and pecans. Pour gelatin mixture into an 8 x 8 x 2 inch baking dish. Let chill until set.

Just before serving, spread sour cream evenly over the top of the gelatin. Cut into squares. Garnish each serving with a pecan half.

Makes 8 servings.

PRETTY IN PINK SALAD

Quick and easy, this dish can be a salad or a dessert.

1 can (21 ounces) cherry filling and topping
1 can(14 ounces) sweetened condensed milk (not evaporated milk)
1 can (8 ounces) crushed pineapple, well-drained
1 cup chopped walnuts
1 container (8 ounces) frozen whipped topping, thawed

In a mixing bowl, combine cherry filling, sweetened condensed milk, pineapple and walnuts; mix well. Gently fold in whipped topping. Spoon into a glass serving bowl or individual parfait glasses. Let chill before serving.

Makes 8 servings.

Serving size: 3/4 cup, 446 calories per serving. Total fat per serving: 21 grams.

Many spices and herbs go well with cherries. Try adding ginger, mustard, cinnamon, thyme, basil, nutmeg or cumin to your favorite recipes.

BLUE CHEESE WALDORF SALAD

Prepare early in the day to blend flavors.

2 medium apples, unpeeled and cubed
2 tablespoons lemon juice
1 cup dried tart cherries
1 cup sliced celery
1/2 cup mayonnaise
1/2 cup slivered almonds
2 tablespoons crumbled blue cheese (about 1/2 ounce)

In a medium serving bowl, toss apple cubes in lemon juice. Add cherries, celery, mayonnaise, almonds and blue cheese; mix well. Refrigerate, covered, to blend flavors.

Makes 6 servings.

Serving size: 2/3 cup, 289 calories per serving. Total fat per serving: 20 grams.

Use an apple variety suitable for salads such as McIntosh, Stayman, Empire, Golden Delicious or Cortland.

CHERRY DREAM SALAD

1 (16 ounce) can dark sweet cherries
1 (16 ounce) can pineapple chunks
1 egg, beaten
2 tablespoons lemon juice
2 tablespoons sugar
Dash salt
1/2 cup sour cream
1/2 cup pecan halves
1 cup miniature marshmallows

Drain cherries and pineapple, reserving 1/4 cup pineapple syrup. In a saucepan, combine egg, pineapple syrup, lemon juice, sugar and salt.

Cook over medium heat, stirring until thick. Remove from heat and fold in sour cream. Cool. Combine with cherries, pineapple, pecans and marshmallows.

Chill one hour or more. Serve in lettuce lined bowl.

Makes 5 - 6 servings.

BUFFET SALAD

Salad:
1 (20 ounce) can crushed pineapple, drained
1/2 cup maraschino cherries, drained
1 (4 ounce) can mandarin oranges, drained
2 apples, diced
3 bananas, sliced
1 cup miniature marshmallows
1/2 cup coconut or nuts, optional

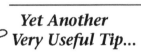

Yet Another Very Useful Tip...

Use a salt shaker filled with powdered or colored sugar for sprinkling cherry cookies. Make the holes larger if needed.

Dressing:
1 cup sugar
2 tablespoons flour
1 egg

Salad:
Drain fruits, reserving 1 cup liquid for dressing. Mix all ingredients together.

Dressing:
Combine sugar and flour in saucepan; add egg and mix. Add 1 cup reserved fruit juices. Cook over low heat or in top of double boiler, stirring constantly, until thick. Cool. Pour over salad and chill. Maintains quality for several days.

BREADS

Cherry Nut Bread

Whole Wheat Cherry Pancakes

Festive Cherry Nut Loaf

Cherry Pecan Pancakes

Cherry Lemon Muffins

Cherry Fruit Bread

Wholesome, Healthy,
Fabulous Breads...

CHERRY–DATE BREAD

1 cup orange juice
1/2 cup water
1 cup dried cherries
1/4 to 1/2 cup chopped dates
1 cup granulated sugar
1 3/4 cups all-purpose flour
1/2 cup soy flour (available at health food stores)
1/2 teaspoon baking powder
1 tablespoon butter, melted
1 egg, slightly beaten
1/2 teaspoon vanilla

In a saucepan, combine orange juice and water. Cook over high heat until boiling. In a heatproof bowl, combine cherries and dates. Pour hot orange juice mixture over fruit; mix well. Set aside. In a large mixing bowl, combine sugar, all-purpose flour, soy flour and baking powder; mix well. In a small container, combine melted butter, egg and vanilla. Add butter mixture and fruit mixture; mix well. Pour batter into a greased 9 x 5 x 3 inch baking pan. Bake in a pre-heated oven at 350 degrees for 45 minutes.

Makes 1 large loaf.

CHERRY DATE NUT BREAD

1 cup hot water
1 cup dates, cut up
1 1/2 cups brown sugar
1 tablespoon butter or margarine, melted
1 egg
1 teaspoon vanilla
2 cups flour
1 teaspoon baking powder
1 teaspoon baking soda
1 cup maraschino cherries, cut up
1/2 cup chopped nuts

Pour hot water over dates; cool. Combine brown sugar, butter, egg, vanilla and dates in water. Sift together flour, baking powder and baking soda; add to first mixture. Fold in cherries and nuts. Pour into greased 8 1/2 x 4 1/2 inch loaf pans. Bake at 350 degrees for 50 - 60 minutes. Cool before slicing.

CHERRY NUT BREAD

2 cups flour
1 cup sugar
1 1/2 teaspoons baking powder
1/4 cup shortening
1 egg, slightly beaten
1/2 cup orange juice

1 tablespoon grated orange peel
2 tablespoons warm water
1/2 cup chopped nuts
1 cup halved tart cherries, well drained

Sift together flour, sugar, and baking powder. Cut in shortening. Stir in egg, orange juice, orange peel, and water. Fold in cherries and pour into greased 8 x 4 x 3 inch loaf pan. Bake for 1 hour at 350 degrees. Cool thoroughly before slicing or wrapping for the freezer.

CHERRY NUT BREAD II

2 1/2 cups flour
1/2 cup sugar
1/2 cup packed brown sugar
3 1/2 teaspoons baking powder
1 teaspoon salt
3 tablespoons vegetable oil
1 1/4 cups milk
1 egg
1/2 teaspoon almond extract
10 ounce jar maraschino cherries, well drained
1 cup crushed almonds

Preheat oven to 350 degrees. Grease bottom of standard loaf pan. Combine all ingredients and mix 30 seconds. Spread batter in pan. Bake 65 - 70 minutes.

> ## More Ideas For Fantastic Baking...
>
> *Cherry fruitcakes will remain moist if you wrap them with a damp towel.*
>
> *To reduce the sugar needed for cake and cookies, try using a small amount of vanilla extract to replace each 1/2 cup of sugar.*
>
> *If you want a moist cake add 2 tablespoons of corn oil to the batter.*
>
> *Never taste the batter when baking, it may contain raw eggs and salmonella contamination.*

WHOLE-WHEAT CHERRY PANCAKES

3/4 cup individually-frozen tart cherries, thawed
3/4 cup all-purpose flour
3/4 cup whole-wheat flour
3 teaspoons baking powder
1/2 teaspoon salt
2 tablespoons honey
1 egg
1 1/4 cup milk

Drain cherries, then cut in half. If necessary,
drain again on paper towels. Set aside.

In a large mixing bowl, combine all-purpose flour, whole-wheat flour, baking
powder and salt; mix well. Add oil, honey, egg and milk; mix just until ingredients
are moistened.

Pour batter on to a hot, greased griddle. Drop 8 - 10 reserved cherry halves on each
pancake. Cook until golden brown, turning once. Makes 15 to 20.

CHERRY COCONUT LOAVES

1 jar (8 ounces) maraschino cherries
3 1/2 cups sifted all-purpose flour
2 teaspoons baking powder
1/8 teaspoon salt
1 1/2 cups light margarine
1 1/2 cups granulated sugar
4 eggs, beaten
2 teaspoons vanilla
1 package (7 ounces) flaked coconut

Drain maraschino cherries, reserving liquid from the jar. Chop cherries; drain again
on paper towels and set aside. Combine flour, baking powder and salt; set aside.

In a large mixing bowl, combine margarine and sugar. Beat with electric mixer on
medium speed until light and fluffy. Add eggs, reserved cherry liquid and vanilla;
mix well. Add flour mixture, mix well. Fold in reserved cherries and coconut. Pour
batter into 2 lightly greased 9 x 5 x 3 inch baking pans. Bake in a preheated 325
degree oven 1 hour, or until done. Makes 2 loaves.

Note: Loaves may be frosted with butter icing or sprinkled with confectioners sugar.

FESTIVE CHERRY NUT LOAF

4 cups all-purpose flour
2 teaspoons baking soda
2 teaspoons baking powder
1/2 teaspoon salt
1 can (21 ounces) cherry filling and topping
2 cups granulated sugar
1/2 cup milk
1 cup chopped walnuts

In a large bowl, combine cherry filling, sugar, oil, eggs (or egg whites) and milk; mix well. Sift together flour, baking soda, baking powder and salt. Add flour mixture to cherry mixture. Mix just until all ingredients are moist. Stir in nuts.

Pour batter into 2 greased and floured 9 x 5 x 3 inch baking pans. Bake in a preheated 350 degree oven 60 to 70 minutes. Let cool 10 minutes; remove from pan. Wrap and store overnight to let flavors develop.

Makes 2 loaves.

Let The Real Fun Begin...

When mixing batter, spray the beaters with Pam before using and the batter won't climb up the beaters.

If you want to prevent a cake from falling after you place the batter in the pan, raise the pan and drop it suddenly to the counter to release the air bubbles.

Canned cherries are only good for 4-5 days in the refrigerator after opening.

Frozen cherries purchased in the supermarket are only good for 2 months in the refrigerator freezer compartment.

CHERRY PECAN PANCAKES

1 1/2 cups milk
1 cup dried tart cherries
3 tablespoons vegetable oil
1 egg, slightly beaten
3 tablespoons honey
2 cups whole-wheat flour
1/4 cup wheat germ, uncooked
1 tablespoon baking powder
1 cup finely chopped pecans

In a medium bowl, combine milk, cherries, oil, egg and honey; mix well. In a large mixing bowl, combine milk mixture into flour mixture. Stir just until all ingredients are moist. Pour 1/4 cup batter on to a preheated griddle. Cook until golden brown, turn only once. Serve immediately with syrup. Makes about 20 pancakes.

Note: If all-purpose flour and toasted wheat germ are substituted for recommended ingredients, milk must be decreased to 1 1/4 cups.

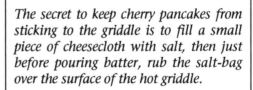

THREE C BREAD (Cherry-Carrot-Coconut Bread)

1 cup vegetable oil
1 1/4 cups granulated sugar
3 eggs
3 cups all-purpose flour
1 teaspoon baking soda
1 teaspoon baking powder
1 teaspoon salt
3 teaspoons ground cinnamon
2 cups finely grated carrots
1 cup flaked coconut
1/2 cup chopped pecans
1 jar (16 ounces) maraschino cherries, drained and cut into quarters

> ### Secrets...Shhh...
>
> *The secret to keep cherry pancakes from sticking to the griddle is to fill a small piece of cheesecloth with salt, then just before pouring batter, rub the salt-bag over the surface of the hot griddle.*
>
> *For the lightest cherry pancakes ever, just use club soda in place of the usual liquid in the batter.*

In a large mixing bowl, combine sugar and oil. Beat with an electric mixer on medium speed until well-mixed. Add eggs; mix well. Combine flour, baking soda, baking powder, salt and cinnamon. Add flour mixture and carrots alternately to sugar mixture. Stir in cherries, pecans and coconut.

Pour batter into 2 greased and floured 9 x 5 x 3 inch baking pans. Bake in a preheated 350 degree oven 50 to 60 minutes, or until wooden pick inserted near center comes out clean. Let cool in pan 5 minutes. Turn onto wire racks to complete cooling. Wrap and refrigerate overnight or until used. Makes 2 loaves.

CHERRY MORNING MUFFINS

1 medium carrot, shredded
1 tart apple, peeled and shredded
1/2 cup dried tart cherries
1/2 cup shredded coconut
1/2 cup chopped pecans
1/2 cup oats, uncooked
1/4 cup wheat germ
1 teaspoon baking soda
3/4 teaspoon ground cinnamon
1/2 teaspoon baking powder
1/4 teaspoon ground ginger
1/2 cup vegetable oil
2 eggs
1/3 cup granulated sugar
2 teaspoon vanilla

In a large bowl, combine carrot, apple, cherries, coconut, and pecans. Combine oatmeal, wheat germ, baking soda, cinnamon, baking powder, salt and ginger. Toss with fruit mixture.

In a small bowl, combine oil, eggs, sugar and vanilla. Stir into carrot mixture; mix until all ingredients are moist. Do not over mix. Pour batter into paper-lined muffin cups, filling 2/3 full. Bake in preheated 375 degree oven 20 minutes, or until tester comes out clean. Makes about 12 muffins.

CHERRY LEMON MUFFINS

2 cups flour
1 teaspoon baking powder
1 teaspoon baking soda
1/4 teaspoon salt
1/4 cup sugar
2 tablespoons honey
2 eggs 1 1/4 cups plain yogurt
1 1/4 cups margarine or butter, melted
1 tablespoon grated lemon zest
1 cup dried Michigan tart cherries

Lemon Syrup:
1/3 cup lemon juice
1/3 cup sugar
3 tablespoons water

Preheat oven to 375 degrees and spray non-stick coating on muffin tins. Combine flour, baking powder, baking soda, salt and sugar. Stir. Combine honey, eggs, yogurt, melted margarine and lemon zest. Stir. Mix dry ingredients with wet ingredients just until evenly moistened. Add dried cherries.

Fill muffin cups 2/3 full. Bake in preheated oven for 15 minutes or until lightly browned. Combine lemon syrup ingredients in a small saucepan. Bring to a boil.

Boil one minute. Prick prepared muffins with a fork 2 - 3 times while in the pan. Drizzle syrup over each hot muffin. Let cool slightly in pan.

CHOC FULL OF CHERRY ORANGE MUFFINS

Zest of 2 oranges plus juice
1/2 cup butter
1 cup sugar
2 eggs
2 cups of all-purpose flour
1 tablespoon baking powder
1/2 teaspoon baking soda
1/2 cup buttermilk
1 cup dried cherries
2 tablespoons Grand Marnier (optional)
3 ounces Hersheys baking chocolate, coarsely chopped
Additional orange juice
Sugar for sprinkling

Place cherries, orange juice and Grand Marnier in saucepan and simmer for five minutes. Drain and reserve remaining juice.

Combine butter, zest, sugar, eggs and juice until creamy. Sift together dry ingredients. Add dry ingredients alternately with buttermilk just until blended. Do not over mix!!! Fold in cherries and chocolate. Spoon into lined muffin tin and bake at 375 degrees for about 30 minutes. Remove from oven and brush tops of muffins with remaining juice and sprinkle with sugar. Cool on rack.

Amazing Cherry Tips To Help You Bake...

The shelf life of a canned dark colored cherry is only 1 year.

Pies should only be kept frozen for 1 year.

Try brushing the bottom crust of cherry pies with egg whites to prevent the fruit juices from soaking in.

To keep your cherry cookies moist, add a teaspoon of jelly to the batter.

CHERRY CHEESE BRUNCH

4 cups baking mix, sifted
1/3 cup sugar
6 tablespoons margarine, melted
2 eggs
1/4 cup milk
Cheese Filling (recipe below)
2 cans (20 ounces) cherry pie filling mixed with 1/4 teaspoon almond extract, or your favorite homemade filling
Frosting (recipe below)

Heat oven to 375 degrees. Grease a 13 x 9 baking pan. Beat eggs slightly with milk in medium bowl. Stir in margarine, baking mix and sugar. Turn dough onto surface dusted with baking mix. Knead lightly 8 to 10 times. Roll dough into rectangle to fit a 13 x 9 baking pan. Spread cream cheese filling on top. Top with cherry pie filling. Bake at 375 degrees for 20 to 25 minutes. Let cool 20 minutes. Drizzle frosting over top.

Cheese Filling:
1 package (8 ounce) cream cheese, softened
2 eggs
1/3 cup sugar
1/2 teaspoon almond extract

Beat all ingredients until smooth.

Frosting:
1 cup sifted powdered sugar
1/4 teaspoon vanilla
1 to 2 tablespoons milk

Serves 15

Freezing Tips...

Freezing Tart Cherries - Wash and pit then pack in a freezer container & cover with a sugar pack:
    Sugar pack - 4 c. water for every 6 c. sugar.
    Cook until syrup is clear then cool.

Freezing Sweet Cherries - Wash and pit then pack into freezer container & cover with syrup pack. Also, add 1/2 tsp. ascorbic acid to every quart of syrup & allow 1/2 inch headspace.
    Syrup pack - 4 c. water for every 6 c. sugar.
    Cook until syrup is clear then cool.

CHERRY FRUIT BREAD

1 1/2 cups vegetable oil
1 1/2 cups sugar
3 eggs, well beaten
2 cups sliced bananas
1 cup dried cherries
1 (8 ounce) can crushed pineapple (undrained)
1 cup chopped walnuts
1 cup coconut
1 1/2 teaspoon vanilla
3 cups flour
1 teaspoon soda
1 teaspoon salt
1 teaspoon cinnamon

Stir until well-blended. Do not beat. Bake in 2 greased loaf pans at 350 degrees for 1 hour or until done. This is a very moist bread, and keeps very well.

CHERRY OATMEAL MUFFINS

Perfect for breakfast-on-the-run or lunchbox treats, these muffins are low in calories.

1 cup old-fashioned or quick cooking oats, uncooked
1 cup all-purpose flour
1/2 cup firmly packed brown sugar
1 1/2 teaspoons baking powder
1/4 teaspoon ground nutmeg
3/4 cup buttermilk
1 egg, slightly beaten
1/4 cup vegetable oil
1 teaspoon almond extract
1 cup frozen tart cherries, coarsely chopped

In a large mixing bowl, combine oats, flour, brown sugar, baking powder and nutmeg. In a small bowl, combine buttermilk, egg, oil and almond extract. Pour buttermilk mixture into oats mixture; stir just to moisten ingredients. Quickly stir in cherries (it is not necessary to thaw cherries before chopping and adding to batter). Spray muffin pan with non-stick spray. Fill muffin cups two-thirds full. Bake in a preheated 400 degree oven 15 to 20 minutes. Makes 12 muffins.

Note: 1 cup canned tart cherries, drained and coarsely chopped, may be substituted for 1 cup frozen tart cherries. *Nutritional information per muffin:* 159 calories, 5.6 grams total fat, 18 mg cholesterol, 61 mg sodium.

COFFEE CAKE MUFFINS

Muffins:
1 1/2 cups all-purpose flour
1/2 cup granulated sugar
2 teaspoons baking powder
1/2 teaspoon salt
1/2 cup vegetable oil
1 egg, slightly beaten
1/3 cup milk
1 teaspoon almond extract

Topping:
1/4 cup firmly packed brown sugar
1/4 cup chopped walnuts
1/4 cup dried cherries
3 tablespoons all-purpose flour
1 tablespoon margarine, melted

Icing:
1/2 cup confectioner's sugar
1 tablespoon milk
1 teaspoon almond extract

To prepare muffins: Combine flour, sugar, baking powder and salt in a mixing bowl. Mix well. In another container, combine oil, egg, milk and almond extract. Stir oil mixture into flour mixture; mix just until ingredients are moistened.

To prepare topping: Combine brown sugar, walnuts, cherries and flour in a small mixing bowl. Stir in melted margarine; mix until crumbly.

To assemble muffins: Use one-half of the muffin batter to fill the bottom of 12 greased muffin cups. Sprinkle one-half of the topping over the batter. Spoon remaining batter over topping. Bake in a preheated 350 degree oven 15 to 20 minutes.

To prepare icing: Combine confectioner's sugar, milk and almond extract in a small bowl. Mix until smooth. Drizzle icing over warm muffins. Makes 12 servings.

LELAND MUFFINS

1 cup dried cherries
Hot water
1 package (18 ounces) spice cake mix
1 egg, slightly beaten
1 cup water
1/3 cup vegetable oil
1 teaspoon baking powder
1 cup chopped pecans
1 container (8 ounces) sour cream

Put cherries into a medium mixing bowl; cover with hot water. Set aside. In a large mixing bowl, combine cake mix, egg, 1 cup water, oil and baking powder; stir until all ingredients are moistened. Do not over mix. Drain off water from cherries; fold cherries and pecans into cake mixture.

Spoon a tablespoon of cake mixture into each of 18 greased muffin cups. Spoon a rounded teaspoon of sour cream on top of cake mixture in muffin cups. Top with remaining cake mixture, filling each cup about two-thirds full. Bake in a preheated 350 degree oven 20 minutes. Makes about 18 muffins.

MICHIGAN CHERRY MUFFINS

1 cup all-purpose flour
3/4 cup oat bran
2/3 cup granulated sugar
1 tablespoon baking powder
1/2 teaspoon salt
3/4 cup skim milk
1/2 cup non-fat yogurt
1/3 cup margarine, melted and cooled
2 egg whites, slightly beaten
1 teaspoon almond extract
3/4 cup dried cherries
1/3 cup chopped pecans
2 teaspoons grated lemon peel

In a medium bowl, combine flour, oat bran, sugar, baking powder and salt. Mix well. In another mixing bowl, combine milk, yogurt, melted margarine, egg whites and almond extract. Stir milk mixture into flour mixture. Mix just until ingredients are moistened. Fold cherries, pecans and lemon peel into batter. Spray muffin cups with non-stick spray. Fill cups two-thirds full with batter. Bake in a preheated 400 degree oven 20 to 25 minutes. Makes 12 to 15 muffins.

CHERRY PUMPKIN MUFFINS

2 1/2 cups flour
1 teaspoon baking soda
3/4 teaspoon salt
1/2 teaspoon cinnamon
1/2 teaspoon nutmeg

3/4 cups chopped cherry nuggets
1/2 cup salad oil
2 eggs
1/3 cup water
1 cup canned pumpkin

Sift together flour, baking soda, salt, cinnamon, nutmeg and sugar; make a well in middle, mix cherry nuggets, oil, eggs, water and pumpkin; pour into "well", stir til dry disappears. Pour into greased muffin tins. Bake at 350 degrees, 25-30 min. Yield: 15 muffins.

CHERRY MUFFINS

3 cups flour
1/2 cup sugar
2 tablespoons baking powder
1 teaspoon salt

2 eggs
1 1/2 cups milk
5 tablespoons melted fat
1 cup tart cherries, drained and halved

Sift together flour, sugar, baking powder, and salt. Beat eggs; add remaining ingredients; blend well. Add to dry ingredients. Stir just until flour disappears, but not until batter is smooth. Fill greased muffin pans 2/3 full, handling the batter as little as possible. Bake 25 - 30 minutes at 400 degrees.

DRIED CHERRY MUFFINS

Topping:
1/4 cup all-purpose flour
1/4 teaspoon ground cinnamon

2 tablespoons granulated sugar
1 tablespoon butter or margarine

Muffins:
2 cups all-purpose flour
1/2 cup granulated sugar
2 teaspoons baking power
1/2 teaspoon baking soda
1/2 teaspoon salt
1/2 cup coarsely chopped pecans

2 eggs
1 cup sour cream
1/3 cup vegetable oil
1/2 cup milk
1 cup dried tart cherries

For the topping, combine flour, sugar and cinnamon in a small bowl; mix well. Cut in butter until mixture resembles coarse crumbs; set aside.

For the muffins, combine flour, sugar, baking powder, baking soda and salt in a large mixing bowl. In another bowl, combine eggs, sour cream, oil and milk; mix well. Add mixture, cherries and pecans to flour mixture; stir only until combined.

Portion batter evenly into 12 paper-lined or lightly greased muffin cups (2 3/4 inches in diameter). Sprinkle reserved crumb topping evenly over batter.

Bake in a preheated 374 degree oven 20 to 25 minutes, or until golden brown. Serve warm. Makes 12 muffins.

Serving size: 1 muffin, 306 calories per serving. Total fat per serving: 15.5 grams.

ALOHA BREAD

Bananas and macademia nuts accented with cherries bring home a tropical taste.

1 jar (10 ounces) maraschino cherries
1 3/4 cups all-purpose flour
2 teaspoons baking powder
1/2 teaspoon salt
1/3 cup butter or margarine, softened
2/3 cup firmly packed brown sugar
2 eggs
1 cup mashed ripe bananas
1/2 cup chopped macademia nuts or walnuts

Drain maraschino cherries, reserving 2 tablespoons juice. Cut cherries in quarters; set aside.

Combine flour, baking powder and salt; set aside.

In a medium mixing bowl, combine butter, 2/3 cup brown sugar, eggs and reserved cherry juice; mix on medium speed of electric mixer until ingredients are thoroughly combined. Add flour mixture and mashed bananas alternately, beginning and ending with flour mixture. Stir in cherries and nuts. Lightly spray a 9 x 5 x 3 inch baking pan with non-stick cooking spray. Spread batter evenly in pan.

Bake in a preheated 350 degree oven 1 hour, or until golden brown and wooden pick inserted near center comes out clean.

Makes 1 loaf, about 16 slices.

Serving size: 1 slice, 185 calories per serving. Total fat per serving: 7.5 grams.

CHERRIES AND CREAM MUFFINS

Bake these muffins and make mouths water.

2 1/2 cups frozen unsweetened tart cherries, divided
1/2 cup butter or margarine
1 cup granulated sugar
2 eggs
1 teaspoon almond extract
1/2 teaspoon vanilla extract
2 cups all-purpose flour
2 teaspoons baking powder
1/2 teaspoon salt
1/2 cup light cream, half-and-half or milk
Granulated sugar

Cut cherries in halves while frozen. Set aside to thaw and drain.

In large mixing bowl, beat butter and sugar until light and fluffy. Add eggs, almond extract and vanilla, beating well. Crush 1/2 cup cherries with a fork; add to batter.

Combine flour, baking powder and salt. Fold in half the flour with a spatula, then half the cream. Add remaining flour and cream. Fold in remaining cherry halves. Portion batter evenly into 12 paper-lined or lightly greased muffin cups (2 3/4 inches in diameter). Sprinkle with sugar.

Bake in a preheated 375 oven 20 to 30 minutes, or until golden brown.

Makes 12 muffins.

Serving size; 1 muffin, 184 calories per serving. Total fat per serving: 10 grams.

Fun Facts About Cherries...

To make a profit from cherry growing it is necessary to produce 2,500-3,000 pounds per acre.

It takes 5-6 yrs. for a tart cherry tree to begin producing a good volume of fruit. Top production is reached in about 10 yrs. and the life of an orchard is about 20-25 yrs.

Sweet cherry trees produce 1,000 pounds per acre at 8-9 yrs. reaching top production at approximately 14 yrs. with an orchard life of 30 yrs.

CHERRY COFFEECAKE

Old-fashioned goodness with everyday ingredients.

Topping:
3/4 cup firmly packed brown sugar
1/2 cup all-purpose flour
1 teaspoon ground cinnamon
1/4 teaspoon ground nutmeg
1/3 cup butter or margarine, softened
1/2 cup old-fashioned or
quick-cooking oats, uncooked

Batter:
1 1/2 cups all-purpose flour
1/2 cup granulated sugar
2 teaspoons baking powder
1/2 teaspoon salt
3 tablespoons butter of margarine
2 eggs
3/4 cup milk 1 can (21 ounces) cherry filling and topping

For the topping, combine sugar, flour, oats, cinnamon and nutmeg in a medium mixing bowl; mix well. Cut in butter to make a crumbly mixture. Set aside.

For the batter, combine flour, sugar, baking powder and salt in a large mixing bowl. Cut in butter until mixture resembles coarse crumbs. Add eggs and milk; mix just until dry ingredients are moistened. Do not over mix; batter will be lumpy. Spread half the batter into a lightly greased 13 x 9 x 2 inch baking pan. Spoon cherry filling evenly over batter. Top with remaining batter. Sprinkle reserved topping over batter.

Bake in a preheated 350 degree oven 30 to 35 minutes, or until golden brown. Serve warm. Makes 12 servings. Serving size: 1 (3 inch) square, 320 calories per serving. Total fat per serving: 9.5 grams.

Two More Freezer Tips...

Freeze whole with stems - pack washed cherries with stems in freezer containers; shake to pack closely, cover & freeze.

Freeze in dry sugar - fill freezer containers with pitted or unpitted cherries and shake to pack closely. Pour 1/3 c. sugar over each pint of cherries then cover tightly & freeze.

RUBY SCONES

Traditional Scottish tea bread updated for the '90's.

1 jar (10 ounces) maraschino cherries
2 cups all-purpose flour
1/4 cup granulated sugar
2 teaspoons baking powder
1/2 cup salt
1/3 cup butter or margarine
1 egg 1/2 cup buttermilk
1/2 cup flaked coconut
1 teaspoon finely chopped crystallized ginger
1 cup confectioner's sugar

Drain cherries, reserving 2 tablespoons juice. Cut cherries into quarters; set aside.

In a large mixing bowl, combine flour, granulated sugar, baking powder and salt. Cut in butter until mixture resembles coarse crumbs. Beat together egg and buttermilk. Add egg mixture, coconut, ginger and drained cherries to flour mixture, stirring with a fork only until combined.

Lightly knead on a floured surface 12 times. Pat or lightly roll dough to 1/2 inch thickness. Cut dough into 8 pieces, using a floured, 4-inch round biscuit cutter. Place rounds on an ungreased baking sheet. Using a sharp, floured knife, cut each scone into four wedges. Do not separate.

Bake in a preheated 400 degree oven 10 to 12 minutes, or until light golden brown.

In a small bowl, combine confectioner's sugar and reserved maraschino cherry juice; mix well. Drizzle over hot scones. Serve warm. Makes 8 (4 inch) scones.

Serving size: 1 scone, 322 calories per serving. Total fat per serving: 10 grams.

Cherries and More Cherries...

If your cherry icing becomes too thick, try adding a few drops of lemon juice and mix well.

When making cherry meringue tortes, always leave the torte in the oven until it's cooled to avoid cracking.

Icing will remain where you put it if you sprinkle the cake first with powdered sugar.

CHERRY BISCOTTI

These twice-baked Italian cookies are perfect for dunking in coffee or milk.

2 cups all-purpose flour
1/2 cup finely chopped walnuts
1 teaspoon baking powder
1/4 teaspoon salt
3/4 cup granulated sugar
2 eggs
1/4 cup vegetable oil
1 tablespoon orange juice
2 teaspoons grated orange peel
1 1/2 teaspoons vanilla extract
1 cup chopped dried tart cherries
1 egg white
1 tablespoon water
Granulated sugar

In a medium mixing bowl, combine flour ,walnuts, baking powder and salt; set aside. In a large mixing bowl, combine sugar and eggs. Beat with an electric mixer at medium speed, scraping bowl often, 2 to 3 minutes, or until thick and pale yellow in color. Add oil, orange juice, orange peel and vanilla; beat 1 to 2 minutes, or until well-mixed. Gradually add flour mixture; mix on low speed 1 to 2 minutes, or until well-mixed. By hand, stir in cherries.

Turn dough onto lightly floured surface (dough will be soft and sticky). Lightly sprinkle with additional flour; knead flour into dough. With floured hands, shape into 2 (8 x 2 inch) logs. Place 3 to 4 inches apart on a greased baking sheet; flatten tops slightly. Combine egg white and water; brush on logs. Sprinkle with sugar.

Bake in a preheated 350 degree oven 25 to 30 minutes, or until lightly browned and firm to the touch. Let cool on baking sheet 15 minutes.

Reduce oven temperature to 300 degrees. With a serrated knife, cut logs diagonally into 1/2 inch slices; arrange slices, cut-side down, on baking sheet. Bake 8 to 10 minutes; turn slices. Bake 8 to 10 minutes, or until golden brown. Remove to wire rack; let cool completely.

Makes about 2 1/2 dozen.

Serving size: 1 cookie, 96 calories per serving. Total fat per serving: 3.5 grams.

CHERRY BANANA BREAD

1 3/4 cups flour
2 teaspoons baking powder
1/4 teaspoon baking soda
1/2 teaspoon salt
1/3 cup shortening

2/3 cup sugar
2 eggs
1 cup mashed ripe bananas
1 cup sliced maraschino cherries

Sift together flour, baking powder, baking soda and salt. Cream shortening. Gradually add sugar; beat until light and fluffy. Add eggs; mix well.

Add dry ingredients alternately with bananas. Fold in cherries. Pour into greased and floured 4 1/2 x 8 1/2 inch pan. Bake at 350 degrees for about one hour. Cool slightly before slicing.

CHERRY FRITTERS

2 cups tart cherries
1 cup flour
1 tablespoon
1 teaspoon baking powder
1/4 teaspoon salt
1/2 cup milk
1 egg

Chop cherries into small bits and drain well. Sift dry ingredients into large bowl. In small bowl mix milk and egg. Add egg mixture and cherries to dry ingredients. Mix only until dry ingredients are moistened. Drop batter by teaspoonsful into 370 degree fat (1 1/2 " deep). Fry until a delicate golden brown. Drain on absorbent paper. Serve sprinkled with sugar or with syrup.

Makes about 30 fritters.

CHERRY BUNS

Filling:
1 (16 ounce) can tart cherries
1/3 cup sugar
2 tablespoons flour
1 tablespoon butter or margarine
Red food coloring

Buns:
1 package active dry yeast
1/4 cup warm water
1 cup milk, scalded
1/2 cup shortening
1/3 cup sugar
1 teaspoon salt
4 to 4 1/4 cups flour
1 egg

Filling:
Drain cherries thoroughly. Combine sugar and flour. Add drained cherries and mix well; cook until thick. Add butter and a few drops of food coloring. Cool.

Buns:
Soften yeast in warm water. Add hot milk to shortening, sugar, and salt. Stir until shortening is melted; cool to lukewarm. Stir in 1 1/2 cups of the flour. Add softened yeast and egg; beat well. Stir in remaining flour or enough to make a soft dough. Cover and let rest 10 minutes. Knead on lightly floured surface until smooth, about 5 minutes. Place in a greased bowl; cover and let rise in a warm place until double in bulk, about 1 to 1 1/2 hours. Punch down; cover and let rest 10 minutes. Roll dough to slightly less than 1/2 inch thick. Cut with a 2 1/2 inch cutter. Place 2 inches apart on a lightly greased baking sheet. Cover and let rise until light, about 45 minutes. With fingers, make a deep depression in the center of buns; fill with cherry filling. Bake at 375 degrees about 15 minutes or until brown.

Makes 1 1/2 dozen buns.

HUNGARIAN CHERRY ROLLS

Sweet Roll Dough:

2 packages active dry yeast	2 eggs
1 teaspoon salt	1/2 cup lukewarm milk
1/2 cup warm water (105-115 degrees)	1/2 cup sugar
1/2 cup shortening, butter or margarine	4 1/2 to 5 cups flour

Dissolve yeast in warm water. Stir in milk, sugar, salt, eggs, shortening and 2 1/2 cups of the flour. Beat until smooth. Mix in enough remaining flour to make dough easy to handle. Turn dough onto lightly floured board; knead until smooth and elastic, about 5 minutes. Put in greased bowl; turn greased side up. Dough can be refrigerated 3 to 4 days. Cover; let rise in warm place (85 degrees) until double in bulk - 1 1/2 hours. Dough is ready if impression remains when touched. Punch down dough.

Cherry Rolls:	1 cup sugar
1/2 cup maraschino or glaze cherries, cut into quarters (about 8 oz. jar)	1 teaspoon cinnamon
	1/2 cup finely chopped
1/2 cup butter or margarine, melted	pecans or other nuts

Grease 10-inch tube pan (if pan has removable bottom, line with foil.) Arrange 1/3 of cherry bits in bottom of pan. Shape pieces of dough into 1 1/2 inch balls. Dip into butter, then into mixture of sugar, cinnamon, and nuts. Arrange a single layer of balls in tube pan so they just touch. Arrange another 1/3 of cherry bits over layer of balls and around edge of pan. Top with another layer of balls. Sprinkle remaining cherry bits over top of second layer of balls. Let rise until double in bulk. Bake at 375 degrees for 35-40 minutes. Loosen from pan. Invert pan onto serving plate so butter-sugar mixture can drizzle down over cake.

To keep a pie crust from becoming soft and soggy during baking, try warming the pan before placing in the undercrust.

Adding a few drops of vinegar to the ice water when making pastry - it will come out flakier.

Cookie dough should be chilled for 15-30 minutes before rolling. This will eliminate the dough from sticking to the rolling pin.

CHERRY FESTIVAL BREAD

1/2 cup flour
1 cup drained, halved maraschino or
    candied cherries
1/2 cup coarsely cut walnuts
2 tablespoons grated orange rind
2 cups flour
3/4 cup sugar

2 teaspoons baking powder
1/2 teaspoon baking soda
3/4 teaspoon salt
3/4 teaspoon salt
3/4 cup milk
1/2 cup whipped cottage cheese
3 tablespoons butter or margarine

Use 1/2 cup flour to coat cherries, walnuts, and orange peel; mix well. Sift together 2 cups flour, sugar, baking powder, baking soda and salt. Mix with milk, cottage cheese and melted butter. Fold in cherry mixture.

Spoon into 2 greased and floured 3 x 7 inch loaf pans or 3 greased and floured No. 2 cans.

Bake at 350 degrees for 50 minutes. Cool for 5 minutes on rack, invert pans and gently shake out; cool on rack.

MAIN COURSES

Spicy Cherry Meatballs

Tangy Cherry Chicken

Cherry Glazed Ham

Pasties with Cherry Pecan Sausage

Cherried Pork Chops

Cherry-Crowned Ham Loaf

Glazed Pork Roast

Oriental Pork

Scrumptious and Delicious
Main Courses...

TANGY CHERRY CHICKEN

1 can (16 ounces) pitted, light sweet cherries (such as Royal Anne)
2 whole chicken breasts, skinned, boned and halved
1/4 cup all-purpose flour
2 teaspoons dry mustard
1/2 teaspoons salt
Dash black pepper
1/4 cup butter or margarine
4 teaspoons brown sugar
2 tablespoons lemon or lime juice, divided
Water
Chopped parsley, for garnish

Drain cherries, reserving liquid. Set aside liquid and cherries while preparing chicken.Using a meat mallet, flatten chicken between 2 pieces of waxed paper. Combine flour, mustard, salt and pepper; mix well. Dredge chicken in seasoned flour; reserve excess flour mixture.

In a large skillet, melt butter. Brown chicken in melted butter. Transfer chicken to a baking dish. Reserve skillet drippings. Top each piece of chicken with one-fourth of the drained cherries, 1 teaspoon brown sugar and 1 teaspoon lemon juice. Bake, uncovered, in a preheated 350 degree oven 20 minutes.

Meanwhile, blend reserved flour mixture into skillet drippings. Add water to reserved cherry liquid to make 1 1/2 cups. Stir liquid mixture into flour mixture. Cook over medium heat until mixture thickens and boils. After chicken cooks 20 minutes, pour thickened sauce over chicken. Bake 5 minutes longer, or until chicken is tender. Before serving, sprinkle chicken with remaining lemon juice and parsley. Makes 4 servings.

Cheery, Cherry Bits & Pieces...

Cherries are Europe's favorite fruit and were once sold by cherry vendors with horse drawn carts.

Cherries came to the mid-west and west coast around 1847 when pioneer horticulturist Henderson Luelling took cherries with him in a covered wagon train to Oregon.

CHERRY GLAZED HAM

3 - 5 pound canned ham
2 tablespoons brown sugar
1/8 teaspoon ground cloves
Pinch of cayenne pepper
1 cup sherry wine or port
1/2 cup chopped nuts, optional
1/2 cup cherry jelly
2 or 3 canned pineapple rings
4 or more maraschino or dark sweet cherries, for garnish

Scrape all the jelly from ham into a 1 quart saucepan. Score ham, bake at 400 degrees for 1 hour. Combine sugar, cloves, cayenne pepper, nuts, wine and half the cherry jelly with the ham jelly in the saucepan over medium heat. Baste ham frequently with this mixture. After the ham has baked the full hour, spread the remaining jelly over the top of ham. Arrange the pineapple rings on top and lay cherries in the center of each ring. Baste and bake 15 minutes to glaze fruit. Remove ham to hot serving platter. Serve basting sauce with ham.

MEXICAN CHERRY CHICKEN

This entree is lowfat.

1/3 to 1/2 cup granulated sugar
2 tablespoons cornstarch
1/2 cup water
1 can (16 ounces) pitted, tart cherries
1 tablespoon almond extract
Dash ground cinnamon
Dash ground cloves
1 cup mild salsa (homemade or store bought)
Salt and black pepper, to taste
Garlic powder, to taste
1 (2 1/2 to 3 pound) chicken, cut up (see note)

In a saucepan, combine sugar and cornstarch. Stir in water (or liquid from cherries). Mix well. Season with salt, pepper and garlic powder to taste.

Put chicken into a 13 x 9 x 2 inch baking pan. Pour cherry sauce over chicken. Bake, covered, in a preheated 350 degree oven 1 hour, or until chicken is tender.

Makes 3 to 4 servings.

Note: 3 chicken leg quarters or 3 whole chicken breasts can be substituted for the whole chicken. Skin and bone chicken, if desired.

PASTIES WITH CHERRY PECAN SAUSAGE

4 cups all purpose flour
2 teaspoons salt
1/2 teaspoon baking powder
1 1/2 cups solid vegetable shortening
10 tablespoons ice water
1 pound sirloin, cut into small pieces
1 pound bulk cherry pecan sausage
5 potatoes, peeled and diced
3 carrots, peeled and finely chopped
1 medium onion, chopped
1 tablespoon salt, or to taste
1 teaspoon ground black pepper

In a large mixing bowl, combine flour salt, baking powder and shortening. Mix by hand until mixture resembles coarse cornmeal. Add ice water all at once; mix just until dough forms a ball. Divide dough into 6 portions; cover and refrigerate. In a large mixing bowl, combine sirloin, sausage, potatoes, carrots, onion, salt and pepper. Mix well to blend ingredients.

On a floured surface, roll one portion of chilled dough into a circle. Place 1 1/2 cups filling on one half of the circle. Fold the other half of the circle over the filling. Seal edges by crimping with a fork. Repeat with remaining dough and filling. Bake in a preheated 400 degree oven 45 minutes, or until golden brown.

Makes 6 large servings.

Facts, Upon Facts, Upon Facts...

When selecting cherries they should be firm and have good color for their variety.

Sweet cherries should always be firm, while tart cherries should be medium firm.

Avoid small immature cherries that have poor color. They will have less juice.

Soft cherries are usually overripe and do not lend themselves well to eating or cooking.

Leave the stems on the cherry and it will stay fresh longer.

Cherries will only last for 2 days in the refrigerator.

CHOCOLATE CHERRY CHICKEN

1 (2 1/2 to 3 pound) chicken, cut up
Flour
Salt and black pepper
2 tablespoons butter
2 tablespoons olive oil
1 1/2 cups chicken broth
1/2 ounce (1/2 square) bittersweet chocolate, melted
1 3/4 cup cherry filling and topping (about 2/3 of a 21 ounce can)
1 cup grated carrots
1/2 cup finely chopped onion
1/2 cup slivered almonds
1/2 teaspoon ground cinnamon
Fresh parsley, for garnish

Dredge chicken in flour. Season with salt and pepper. In a large skillet, heat butter and olive oil. Brown chicken in oil mixture. Place chicken in a 13 x 9 x 2 inch baking pan.

Add 2 tablespoons flour to drippings in skillet. Cook over medium heat, stirring constantly, until brown. Add chicken broth. Cook over medium heat until thickened and bubbly. Remove from heat; stir in chocolate, cherry filling, carrots, onions, almonds and cinnamon. Mix well. Pour sauce over chicken. Bake covered, in a preheated 325 degree oven 1 hour, or until chicken is tender.

Makes 4 servings.

CHERRIED PORK CHOPS

4-6 pork chops
1/2 cup sherry
4 teaspoons paprika
2/3 cup flour
2 tablespoons shortening
1 tablespoon cornstarch
1/2 cup brown sugar
1/2 cup lemon juice
1 (16 ounce) can dark sweet cherries
1 clove garlic, crushed
1 teaspoon ginger
1 teaspoon basil
1 teaspoon oregano
2 teaspoons salt
2 oranges, peeled and sliced

Trim chops of excess fat. Marinate chops in wine one hour; drain, reserving wine.

Trim chops of excess fat. Marinate chops in wine one hour; drain, reserving wine. Season chops with paprika; dip in flour; brown in shortening. Drain excess fat. Combine cornstarch, brown sugar, wine and lemon juice to make a smooth paste. Add undrained cherries, garlic, spices and salt; blend well. Pour over chops. Cover skillet and cook slowly 30 to 45 minutes until meat is tender.

Serve chops over rice. Garnish with orange slices, if desired.

HEARTY SPICED CHERRY CASSEROLE

3/4 cup all-purpose flour
2 teaspoons dried parsley flakes
1/2 teaspoon dried thyme
1/2 teaspoon meat tenderizer
1/2 teaspoon salt
1/4 teaspoon ground nutmeg
1/4 teaspoon ground black pepper
2 pounds venison or lean beef, cut into bite-sized pieces
Vegetable oil
1 large onion, cut into eighths
1 clove garlic, minced
3/4 cup water
1/2 cup cherry wine (or red wine)
1 teaspoon Worcestershire sauce
2 carrots, sliced into 1/2 pieces
2 medium potatoes, peeled and cut into fourths
3/4 cup pitted, tart cherries (about 1/2 of a 16 ounce can)
1/2 cup chopped celery
1/2 cup sliced mushrooms
1/4 cup maple syrup
3/4 teaspoon curry powder

In a plastic bag or other container, combine flour, parsley, thyme, meat tenderizer, salt, nutmeg and black pepper. Put venison or beef cubes in bag; shake until coated. Add a small portion of vegetable oil to a large skillet. Brown meat in skillet. Remove meat from skillet and place in a 3 quart baking dish. Add onion and garlic to meat. In a small bowl, combine water, wine and Worcestershire sauce. Pour over meat. Bake uncovered, in a preheated 325 degree oven 1 hour.

Remove casserole from oven. Add carrots, potatoes, cherries, celery, mushrooms, maple syrup and curry powder. Stir to blend ingredients. Cover and return to a 325 degree oven. Bake 1 1/2 hours, or until vegetables are tender.

Makes 6 to 8 servings.

Note: Fresh morel mushrooms, when in season, are an extra special addition to this casserole.

SMOKEY TURKEY CUTLETS WITH CHERRY RIESLING SAUCE

4 turkey cutlets (6 ounces each)
4 teaspoons liquid smoke
4 teaspoons water
2 cups plus 2 tablespoons Cherry Riesling wine (or other blush wine), divided
1/2 cup dried tart cherries
2 teaspoons cornstarch
1/2 teaspoon grated orange or lemon peel
2 tablespoons honey
Wild rice seasoned with rosemary (optional)

Place turkey cutlets in a shallow bowl (or a large plastic bag). Pour liquid smoke and water over cutlets. Let marinate in refrigerator 20 minutes.

Meanwhile, in a large saucepan, combine 2 cups wine and dried cherries. Cook over high heat until liquid is reduced by one half. In a small container, combine remaining 2 tablespoons wine and cornstarch; mix until smooth. Stir into wine mixture; cook over medium heat until thickened. Add orange peel and honey to sauce. Keep warm.

Broil cutlets 4 to 5 inches from heat 12 to 15 minutes, or until cutlets are done. Place broiled cutlets on warm serving plates. Pour about 1/4 cup wine sauce over each cutlet. Serve with wild rice, if desired.

Makes 4 servings.

Note: Smoked pork chops can be substituted for turkey cutlets. Do not marinate in liquid smoke. Broil, bake or grill chops until tender. Serve as directed above with wine sauce.

CHERRY COUNTRY MEATBALLS

3 pounds Plevalean (91 % lean ground beef with cherries)
1 1/2 cups dry bread crumbs
1 cup finely chopped onion
1/3 cup dry milk powder
1/4 cup milk
3 eggs
3 tablespoons dried parsley
1 tablespoon Worcestershire sauce
1 1/2 teaspoons salt
1/4 teaspoon black pepper
Cherry tomato Sauce (recipe in Sauce section)

In a large mixing bowl, combine Plevalean®, bread crumbs, onion, milk powder, milk, eggs, parsley, Worcestershire sauce, salt and pepper; mix well. Shape into 1 inch balls. Place meatballs in a single layer in a greased shallow baking pan. Bake in a preheated 400 degree oven 12 minutes, or until lightly browned.

Meanwhile prepare Cherry Tomato Sauce. Remove meatballs from oven and put in a large casserole. Pour Cherry Tomato Sauce over meatballs. Bake covered, in a preheated 350 degree oven 45 minutes, or until hot and bubbly. Stir meatballs once during baking time. Makes 6 dozen meatballs; enough for 12 to 15 servings.

SPICY CHERRY CHICKEN

A lowfat main course

2 1/2 to 3 pound chicken legs and thighs, skinned
Seasoned salt
2 tablespoons vegetable oil
1 jar (12 ounces) cherry preserves
2 tablespoons lemon juice
4 whole cloves
1/4 teaspoon salt
1/4 teaspoon ground allspice
1/4 teaspoon ground mace
Cooked rice

Sprinkle chicken with seasoned salt. In large skillet, heat oil. Add chicken; cook to brown on all sides. Remove chicken from skillet; drain fat from skillet. In a small bowl, combine cherry preserves, lemon juice, cloves, salt, allspice and mace. Return chicken to skillet. Pour cherry sauce over chicken. Simmer, covered, 1 hour, or until chicken is tender. Serve hot with rice. Makes 6 to 8 servings.

CHERRY-CROWNED HAM LOAF

1 1/2 cups dry bread crumbs
1/2 cup milk
1 pound ground ham
1 pound ground pork shoulder
2 tablespoons chopped onion
1/3 cup snipped fresh parsley
1 teaspoon dry mustard
2 eggs, beaten
1 can (16 ounces) tart cherries
4 teaspoons cornstarch
2 tablespoons granulated sugar
1/4 teaspoon salt
1/8 teaspoon ground cinnamon
1/8 teaspoon grated nutmeg
1/4 teaspoon red food coloring

In a large mixing bowl, combine bread crumbs and milk. Add ham, pork, onion, parsley, mustard and eggs; mix well. Pack meat mixture into a 1 1/2 quart round baking dish. Bake in a preheated 350 degree oven 1 hour. Drain cherries, reserving juice. Add enough water to juice to measure 1 cup liquid. Place juice in a saucepan; stir in cornstarch, sugar , salt, cinnamon and nutmeg.

Cook over medium heat, stirring constantly, until thickened and clear. Add cherries and food coloring; cook until heated through. Drain any drippings from ham loaf and unmold on serving platter. Top with small amount of cherry sauce. Serve with remaining sauce. Makes 8 servings.

CHICKEN CHERRY SALAD

2 cups individually quick frozen tart cherries, thawed
4 cups cooked chicken, cubed
1 cup sliced celery
3/4 cup slivered almonds
1/3 cup mayonnaise
1 cup frozen non-dairy whipped topping, thawed
Salt and pepper, to taste
Lettuce leaves, rinsed and well-drained

Drain cherries. In a large mixing bowl, combine cherries, chicken, celery and almonds. in a small bowl, combine whipped topping and mayonnaise. Fold topping mixture into chicken mixture.

Serve on lettuce. Makes 6 servings.

CHERRY PASTA WITH SAUTEED DUCK OR CHICKEN BREAST IN CHERRY PORT SAUCE

Pasta:
1 pound of all purpose flour
5 - 6 eggs
1 cup pureed dry - tart cherries
1- 2 tsp red food coloring
pinch of salt
1/2 - 2 tsp cinnamon

Mix eggs and red food coloring with whisk. Sift together salt, cinnamon, and flour. Combine all ingredients in mixing bowl and knead until smooth. Cover and let sit for 30 min. Put dough through pasta machine or hand cut to desired length and size. Boil in salted water until tender but not soft. Makes about 1 1/2 lbs. pasta.

Duck or Chicken Breast:
4 (4 - 5 ounce) duck or chicken breasts

Marinate in cranberry or cherry juice with 1/4 cup dried cherries for about 3 or 4 hours. Sautee breasts in pan with about 3 tsp. olive oil until breasts are nicely browned. Remove breasts, place on baking sheet; bake at 325 degrees for 15 minutes.

Cherry Port Sauce:
1/4 cup port wine
Cranberry or cherry juice
2 cups brown stock (or Demi-glace for a richer sauce)
1/2 cup dried tart cherries (or just use cherries from marinade)
2 tsp flour, plus
2 teaspoons butter, to make Buerre Manie used as thickener for sauce.

Add port wine to pan used to sautee breasts and reduce to medium heat. Add stock, juice, and dried cherries and simmer for 5 minutes. Continue to reduce heat and then add Buerre Manie to desired thickness. Add 1/2 cup sugar for a sweeter pasta.

Notes From The Chef...

Maraschino cherries were first produced in Italy, when a sweet white cherry was soaked in a cordial called "maraschino," which was produced from another cherry called the Marasca Cherry. The French actually gave it the name "Maraschino Cherry".

Sweet cherries are usually available from May-August. Tart cherries are available from June-August.

CHERRY BACON OPEN-FACED SANDWICHES

8 slices Canadian bacon sliced 1/4 inch thick
4 English muffins, split
8 slices pineapple (one 16 ounce can) drain and reserve juice
8 slices Amish Swiss cheese
Cherry sauce (recipe below)

Panbroil Canadian bacon on both sides. Top muffin halves with bacon. Top each with one slice of pineapple and slice of cheese. Boil sandwiches until cheese melts. Top with warm cherry sauce. Serve immediately.

Cherry Sauce:
1 cup cherry juice
1/2 cup pineapple juice
2 tablespoons sugar
1 tablespoon lemon juice
1/2 teaspoon dried tarragon
5 whole cloves
2 tablespoons water
1 tablespoon cornstarch
3/4 cup dried cherries

Mix first six ingredients. Simmer 10 minutes. Strain cloves and tarragon. Mix water and cornstarch and stir into strained juice. Cook until thickened. Add dried cherries. Cook on low heat until cherries are heated through. Divide evenly among 8 sandwiches. Serve immediately.

GLAZED PORK ROAST

Roast:
4 pound boneless pork loin roast, rolled

Cherry Glaze:
12 ounces cherry preserves
2 tablespoons light corn syrup
1/4 cup red wine vinegar
1/4 teaspoon salt
1/4 teaspoon cinnamon
1/4 teaspoon nutmeg
1/4 teaspoons cloves
1/4 cup slivered almonds

Roast:
Insert meat thermometer into center of thickest muscle of pork loin. Roast loin, fat side up, at 325 degrees until meat thermometer reads 150 degrees. Glaze with cherry glaze and continue cooking until meat thermometer reads 170 degrees.

Cherry Glaze:
In saucepan, combine all ingredients except almonds. Cover and cook on low heat for about four minutes. Remove cover; stir and cook 2 minutes more. Add toasted almonds. Spoon enough cherry almond sauce over pork to glaze. Serve remaining sauce with roast.

ORIENTAL PORK

1 pound boneless pork
3 tablespoons soy sauce
3 tablespoons white vinegar
2 cloves garlic, chopped
1 tablespoon vegetable oil
1 can (21 ounces) cherry filling and topping
1 can (8 ounces) pineapple chunks, drained
1/4 pound snow peas, trimmed and cut in half
2 tablespoons toasted sesame seeds (optional)
Hot, cooked rice

Trim all visible fat from pork and cut into 3/4-inch cubes. Put pork in a 2 quart microwave-safe dish. Combine soy sauce, vinegar and garlic; pour over pork. Marinate pork in sauce about 1 hour, turning cubes often.

Preheat a 10-inch microwave browning dish on HIGH (100% power) 5 minutes. Add oil, swirl to coat dish. Remove pork from marinade, reserving for later use. Add drained pork to browning dish. Microwave, uncovered, on HIGH 3 to 4 minutes, or until pork is no longer pink. Remove pork with a slotted spoon; set aside.

Add cherry filling to the soy sauce marinade, using the same 2 quart microwave-safe dish used to marinate the pork cubes. Mix well.

Then add cooked pork, pineapple and snow peas. Stir to combine. Cover dish with waxed paper. Microwave on HIGH 5 minutes (stirring and turning dish twice) or until mixture is hot.

Sprinkle with toasted sesame seeds, if desired. Serve over rice.

Makes 4 servings.

CHERRY CHICKEN ALMOND CASSEROLE

5 cups diced, cooked chicken breast
2 cups diced celery
3 cups cooked rice
1 (8 ounce) can sliced water chestnuts
2 can cream of chicken soup
1/2 cup sour cream
1/2 cup mayonnaise
2 tablespoons chopped onions
2 tablespoons lemon juice
1 tablespoon salt
3/4 teaspoon white pepper
1/2 cup dried cherries
1 cup sliced almonds

Mix above ingredients and put into
buttered 9 x 13 inch pan.

Topping:
1/2 cup sliced almonds
3 cups crumbled corn flakes
2/3 cup butter

Mix above ingredients and sprinkle on top of casserole. Bake at 350 degrees for 35 - 45 minutes.

Cherry Facts You Should Know...

If prepared for freezing, cherries will last for 2 months in the freezer compartment of a refrigerator.

When storing cherries, never wash them. Place them loosely in a shallow container.

In a zero degree freezer they will last for 1 year.

The shelf life of a canned light-colored cherry is 3 years.

One quart with stems = 1 1/2 pounds = 3 cups, stemmed and pitted or 2 cups of juice.

One quart stemmed = 2 pounds = 4 cups, pitted or 2 cups juice.

BRUNCH PIE

2 cups individually quick-frozen tart cherries, chopped
1/2 pound bulk pork sausage, crumbled
1/2 cup chopped pecans
1 1/2 cups shredded Monterey Jack cheese, divided
6 eggs
1/2 cup milk
1 tablespoon all-purpose flour
Salt and pepper, to taste

In a 2 quart microwave-safe bowl, combine cherries, sausage and pecans. (Cherries do not need to be thawed before chopping and using in this recipe.) Microwave, covered, on HIGH (100% power) 2 minutes. Stir and break up sausage pieces. Microwave, covered, on HIGH 2 to 3 minutes more, or until sausage is cooked.

Drain juices from sausage mixture. Stir in 1/2 cup cheese. Spread sausage mixture evenly in a lightly greased 9-inch round microwave-safe pie plate. Set aside In a microwave-safe bowl; combine eggs, milk and flour. Season with salt and pepper. Microwave, uncovered, on HIGH 3 minutes (beating vigorously with a wire whisk 3 times during cooking), or until two-thirds of egg mixture is cooked.

Stir remaining 1 cup cheese into egg mixture; mix well. Pour egg mixture over sausage mixture. Microwave, covered, on HIGH 4 to 5 minutes (rotating one-half turn after 2 minutes), or until eggs are set in the middle.

Let cool, covered, 5 minutes before serving. Refrigerate any unused portions.

Makes 6 servings.

Note: 1 can (16 ounces) pitted tart cherries, well-drained and chopped, may be substituted for 2 cups frozen tart cherries.

CHERRY BRUNCH PIE II

Serve with a mixed green salad.

1/2 pound bulk sausage
1 can (16 ounces) unsweetened tart cherries, drained and coarsely chopped
1 cup shredded sharp Cheddar cheese (about 4 ounces)
1 cup buttermilk baking mix
1 teaspoon dried basil
1/2 teaspoon ground black pepper
4 eggs, slightly beaten
1 1/2 cups milk

In a large skillet, cook sausage until brown, breaking into small pieces as it cooks;

drain off fat. Remove from heat. Add cherries; mix well. Spoon sausage mixture into a 10-inch deep-dish pie plate. Top with cheese.

In a medium mixing bowl, combine baking mix, basil, salt and pepper. Add eggs and milk; beat until smooth. Pour over cheese. Bake in a preheated 400 degree oven 35 to 40 minutes, or until a knife inserted in center comes out clean. Let cool 5 minutes. Cut into wedges. Serve immediately.

Makes 6 servings.

Note: 1 1/2 cups frozen unsweetened tart cherries can be substituted for canned cherries. Partially thaw cherries, then coarsely chop and drain before adding to sausage.

Serving size: 1 wedge, 428 calories per serving. Total fat per serving: 30 grams.

TART AND TASTY STUFFING

Brighten traditional bread stuffing with cherries.

2 tablespoons butter or margarine
3/4 cup chopped celery
1/2 cup chopped onion
1 teaspoon dried thyme
1/4 teaspoon poultry seasoning
1 package (7 ounces) dried herb-seasoned stuffing cubes
3/4 cup chicken broth
2 cups frozen unsweetened tart cherries, thawed and drained

Melt butter in a medium saucepan over medium heat. Add celery and onion; cook 2 to 3 minutes, or until vegetables are tender. Stir in thyme and poultry seasoning.

In a large bowl, toss together celery mixture, stuffing cubes and broth. Gently stir in cherries. Spoon into a lightly greased 2 quart casserole.

Bake, covered, in a preheated 350 degree oven 30 minutes, or until mixture is hot. (Or use to stuff a 12 pound turkey.)

Makes 6 servings.

Note: 1 can (16 ounces) unsweetened tart cherries, well-drained, can be substituted for frozen tart cherries.

Serving size: 3/4 cup, 122 calories per serving. Total fat per serving: 7 grams.

BEEF BURGUNDY

For everyday dinners or special occasions, beef takes on
new flavors with mushrooms, onions and cherries.

2 1/2 pounds boneless beef round steak
4 cloves garlic, minced
1/2 cup chopped onion
2 cups Burgundy or other dry red wine
1 can (10 3/4 ounces) condensed cream of mushroom soup, undiluted
1 1/2 cups dried tart cherries
2 jars (4 1/2 ounces each) button mushrooms, drained
1 cup pearl onions (fresh, frozen or canned)
3 tablespoons all-purpose flour
1/2 cup water
1 package (12 ounces) medium egg noodles, cooked and well drained

Trim fat from steak; cut steak into 1 inch cubes. Coat a large, oven-proof Dutch oven or stockpot with non-stick cooking spray; place over medium heat until hot. Add steak; cook, stirring occasionally, 8 to 10 minutes, or until meat is browned. Drain well; set aside.

Re-coat pan with cooking spray; place over medium heat. Add garlic and chopped onion; cook 1 minute. Add wine and mushroom soup; mix well. Bring mixture to a boil. Return steak to pan; stir in cherries, mushrooms and pearl onions.

In a small bowl, combine flour and water, blending until smooth with a wire whisk. Gradually stir flour mixture into steak mixture; mix well. Bake, covered, in a preheated 350 degree oven 1 1/2 hours, or until steak is tender and mixture is thickened. Serve over cooked noodles.

Makes 8 servings.

Serving size: 3/4 cup, 528 calories per serving. Total fat per serving: 12 grams.

CHERRY CHICKEN WITH APRICOT SAUCE

For a simple dinner, grill or broil chicken and top with this tangy sauce.

6 chicken breast halves, skinned and boned
1/12 cups apricot nectar
1 tablespoon red wine vinegar
1 tablespoon brown sugar
1 tablespoon Dijon-style mustard
1 cup dried tart cherries
1 can (17 ounces) apricot halves, drained and cut into wedges

Cook chicken on gas or charcoal grill, under the broiler, or on top of the stove. Season, as desired; keep warm.

In a large skillet, combine apricot nectar, vinegar, brown sugar and mustard; mix well. Add cherries. Bring to a boil. Reduce heat; simmer 10 minutes. Add apricot wedges; simmer 5 minutes, or until sauce thickens. Serve sauce over chicken.

Makes 6 servings.

Serving size: 1 chicken breast half, 234 calories per serving. Total fat per serving: 1 gram

BEEFY BAKED BEANS

One-dish meal is perfect for potlucks, family gatherings or camping.

1 pound lean ground beef
2 cans (16 ounces each) pork and beans in tomato sauce
1 can (15 ounces) kidney beans
1 cup ketchup
1 envelope (1 3/8 ounces) dry onion soup mix
1/2 cup water
2 tablespoons prepared yellow mustard
2 teaspoons cider vinegar
2 cups frozen unsweetened tart cherries

In a skillet over medium heat, cook ground beef until browned. Drain fat.

Add pork and beans, kidney beans, ketchup, dry onion soup mix, water, mustard and vinegar to meat; mix well. Stir in cherries (it is not necessary to thaw them). Pour meat mixture into a 2 1/2 quart baking dish. Bake in a preheated 400 degree oven 30 minutes, stirring occasionally. Serve hot.

Makes 8 servings.

Note: 1 cup dried tart cherries can be substituted for frozen tart cherries.

Serving size: 1 cup, 383 calories per serving. Total fat per serving: 14 grams.

CHERRY DELICIOUS RIBS

A tasty departure from tomato-based barbecue sauce.

8 pounds pork spareribs
1 can (21 ounces) cherry filling and topping
1/2 cup chopped onion
2 tablespoons olive oil
1/4 cup soy sauce
2 teaspoons spicy brown mustard
1 teaspoon ground ginger
1 teaspoon Worcestershire sauce

Cut ribs into serving portions of 2 or 3 ribs each. In a large saucepot or Dutch oven, simmer ribs, covered, in salted water 45 to 50 minutes, or until tender; drain.

In an electric blender or food processor container, purée cherry filling until smooth.

In a large saucepan, cook onion in olive oil until tender. Add puréed cherry filling, soy sauce, mustard, ginger, and Worcestershire sauce; mix well. Simmer, uncovered 10 to 15 minutes, stirring occasionally.

Place ribs on gas grill over low heat or on charcoal grill 4 to 6 inches from slow coals. Turn ribs 3 or 4 times and brush frequently with sauce. Cook 25 minutes, or until done; discard any remaining sauce.

Makes 8 servings.

Serving size: 2 to 3 ribs, 461 calories per serving. Total fat per serving: 28 grams.

BEEF CHERRY-YAKI

For busy schedules, stir-fry is an easy solution.

3/4 pound boneless beef sirloin steak
1 1/2 cups frozen unsweetened tart cherries
1/3 cup soy sauce
1/4 cup plus 1 tablespoon canola oil, divided
3 tablespoon honey
1/2 teaspoon ground ginger
1 clove garlic, minced
1 tablespoon cornstarch
2 medium carrots, julienne sliced
6 green onions, sliced
1 can (4 ounces) sliced water chestnuts, drained
Hot cooked rice

Partially freeze meat. Thinly slice across the grain into bite-size strips; set aside. Thaw cherries; drain, reserving juice in a shallow dish, combine soy sauce, 1/4 cup oil, honey, ginger and garlic; mix well. Add beef strips. Refrigerate, covered 1 hour, stirring once. Remove meat from marinade; discard marinade.

Add enough water to reserved cherry juice to make 1/4 cup. In a small bowl, combine juice and cornstarch; mix well.

Heat remaining 1 tablespoon oil in a skillet over medium heat. Add carrots and onions. Cook until tender crisp; remove from skillet. (Add more oil, if necessary.) Add meat; cook until brown. Remove meat. Stir cornstarch mixture; add to skillet. Cook, stirring, until thickened and bubbly. Return vegetables and meat to skillet; add cherries and water chestnuts. Cook, stirring often, 5 minutes, or until hot. Serve over rice.

Makes 6 servings.

Serving six: 3/4 cup, 239 calories per serving. Total fat per serving: 9 grams.

CHERRY BLUE CHEESE SANDWICH

6 1 inch slices French bread
3 ounces blue cheese, softened
4 ounces Lite-cream cheese, softened
1 tablespoon water
1 tablespoon mayonnaise or salad dressing
1/2 teaspoon onion powder
6 strips crisp bacon, crumbled
1 cup cherry preserves

Toast one side of French bread slices under broiler. Cream blue cheese, cream cheese, water, mayonnaise and onion powder until smooth. Spread on untoasted sides of bread. Broil until bubbly. Sprinkle crumbled bacon over slices. Spread with cherry preserves as served.

CHERRY CHICKEN SALAD

2 cups diced cooked chicken or turkey
1 cup diced celery
2 tablespoons minced pimento
3/4 teaspoon salt
1/2 cup coarsely chopped walnuts
1 cup drained and halved dark sweet cherries
1/2 cup drained pineapple tidbits
1 tablespoon lemon juice
2 tablespoons French dressing
1/2 cup Lite-mayonnaise or salad dressing

Toss together all of the ingredients.
Serve on a lettuce leaf.

Makes 6 or 8 servings.

CHICKEN SOUTH PACIFIC

1 broiler chicken, cut in serving pieces
1/4 cup oil
1 (16 ounce) can tart cherries
1 tablespoon cornstarch
1 tablespoon soy sauce
1 tablespoon vinegar
1 tablespoon sugar
3/4 cup quick cooking rice
1/4 cup blanched almonds
3/4 cup raisins
1/4 teaspoon salt
1 onion, sliced in rounds
1 green pepper, sliced in rounds

Brown and cook chicken in hot oil in frying pan. Drain off oil; remove chicken to serving platter in warm oven. Drain cherries, reserving juice. Combine juice, cornstarch, soy sauce, vinegar and sugar. Cook in frying pan, stirring until mixture is slightly thickened; cover pan and simmer 10 minutes. Stir in rice, cherries, almonds, raisins, salt and onion. Bring mixture to a boil; cover and simmer 10 minutes. Spoon over chicken. Garnish with green pepper. Serve immediately.

HOLIDAY CHERRY CHICKEN

Chicken:
1 (2 1/2 - 3 pound) chicken, cut in pieces
3 tablespoons butter or margarine, melted
Salt
Pepper
Paprika

Cherry Sauce:
16 ounce can tart cherries
1/2 cup sugar
6 drops red food coloring, optional
2 tablespoons cornstarch
1/2 cup chicken broth
1 unpeeled orange, sliced and quartered
1/2 cup slivered almonds

Chicken:
Put chicken, with skin removed, on a
cold broiler rack. Brush with melted
butter and sprinkle with salt, pepper and paprika. Broil on low heat for 10 minutes.
Turn and brush with melted butter and sprinkle with salt, pepper and paprika.
Continue cooking 35 to 45 minutes or until done, turning every 10 minutes. Note:
Chicken can be pre-cooked according to your preference.

Cherry Sauce:
Reserve 1/4 cup cherry juice. Put cherries and remaining juice in a saucepan. Add
sugar and food coloring and heat to boiling. Combine reserved juice and
cornstarch, stir into the sauce along with the 1/2 cup of broth, and cook until
thickened and thick. Add orange pieces and almonds. Put chicken in skillet; add
sauce and simmer 5 to 10 minutes. Garnish with orange slices and toasted
almonds, if desired.

SUPREMES AUX CERISES

2 whole chicken breasts, skinned and split
3 tablespoons butter or margarine
3 tablespoons brandy
1 small clove garlic, minced
1 (4 ounce) can sliced mushrooms, drained
1 tablespoon cornstarch or potato starch
1/2 teaspoon bottled browning and seasoning base
1 1/4 cup chicken broth
1/4 cup white wine (dry)
1 cup well-drained dark sweet cherries (fresh, canned or frozen)
Salt to taste
Pepper to taste

Brown chicken breast halves slowly in butter. Heat brandy; ignite and pour over chicken. Remove to a platter. Add garlic and mushrooms to drippings in skillet; saute several minutes. Combine starch, browning and seasoning base, cold chicken broth and wine. Slowly stir into skillet. Cook and stir until sauce bubbles and thickens. Add chicken and cherries. Season to taste with salt and pepper. Cover and cook slowly until chicken is tender, about 10 to 15 minutes longer. Serve immediately.

CHERRY SAUCED PORK BALLS

Meatballs:
1 pound lean ground pork
1/2 cup sort bread crumbs
1 egg
1 1/2 tablespoons minced onion
1/4 cup finely chopped water chestnuts
2 tablespoons milk
1 teaspoon Worcestershire sauce
3/4 teaspoon salt
1/4 teaspoon garlic salt
Dash pepper
2 tablespoons butter or margarine

Cherry Sauce:
1 (16 ounce) can cherries
1 tablespoon cornstarch
1 tablespoon firmly packed brown sugar
1/2 teaspoon grated orange peel
1/4 cup orange juice
3 tablespoons vinegar
3 tablespoons soy sauce
1/4 teaspoon Worcestershire sauce

Meatballs:
Combine all ingredients except butter. Shape into balls and brown in butter. Drain; remove to casserole.

Cherry Sauce:
Drain cherries, reserving juice; dissolve cornstarch in cherry juice. Combine all ingredients in saucepan. Cook, stirring constantly, until thick and clear. Add cherries. Pour over meatballs; bake at 350 degrees for 30 minutes. Serve over rice, if desired.

PORK AND CHERRY JUBILANT

Pork Cutlets:
6 boneless pork cutlets
1/2 cup flour
1 egg, beaten
1/4 cup milk
2 cups fine, soft bread crumbs
1 1/2 teaspoons sage
3/4 teaspoon celery salt
3/4 teaspoon onion salt
1/3 cup oil or shortening

Cherry Sauce:
1 (16 ounce) can dark sweet cherries
1/4 cup water
1/4 cup cornstarch
1 teaspoon salt
1 tablespoon butter or margarine
2 tablespoons brandy, optional

Pork Cutlets:
Dredge meat with flour. Combine egg and milk. Dip meat in egg mixture. Mix bread crumbs, sage, celery salt, and onion salt together. Roll cutlets in bread crumb mixture. Preheat electric fry pan to 350 degrees. Add oil; brown breaded pork cutlets well on both sides. Reduce heat to 225 degrees and cover pan. Cook for 15 minutes, or until pork is thoroughly cooked. If desired, remove cover and increase heat to 375 degrees for a few minutes to re-crisp the bread coating.

Cherry Sauce:
Drain syrup from cherries into saucepan; add jelly. Heat to melt jelly. Combine water and cornstarch mixture to cherry syrup mixture and cook until thick and clear, stirring constantly. Add salt, butter and brandy. Stir in cherries. Serve over pork cutlets.

Check These Tidbits Out...

The earliest known statement regarding cherries was made in 300 B.C., when the Greek, Theophrastus "Father of Botany" described the fruit.

2/3 cup of fresh sweet cherries = 80 calories.

An easy formula for a great cherry cake flour is to mix together 2 tablespoons of cornstarch in 1 cup of all-purpose flour.

Never squeeze out the cherry pit as this will cause an excess amount of juice loss and "cherry collapse" may occur.

DESSERTS

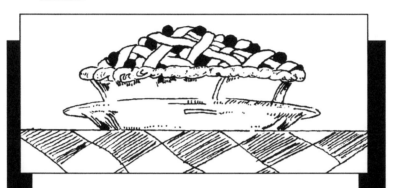

Frozen Cherry Cordial Pie

Cherry Cheese Cake

Cherry Angel Dessert

Cherry Mocha Mousse Pie

Santa's Cherry Ring

Jewish Coffee Cake

Fruit Fluff

Chocolate Cherry Terrine

Cherry Melting Moments Cookies

And Many More Delicious Desserts...

CHERRY CHEESE CAKE

8 oz. package of cream cheese
1 1/4 cups of finely crushed graham crackers (15 squares)
20 oz. can of cherry pie filling
1 cup and 2 tablespoon powdered sugar
1/3 cup melted butter or margarine
2 cartons whipped cream
9-inch pie pan

CRUST:
Mix the finely crushed graham crackers with 2 tablespoons of powdered sugar and the margarine. Line the pan with the crust mix and press firmly. Bake at 350 degrees for 12-15 minutes.

FILLING:
Mix the cream cheese with one cup of powdered sugar (better if sifted), and one carton of whipped cream. Spread the mixture over the cooled crust. After the filling is spread, cover the cake with the can of cherries.

Note: 1 can (16 ounces) tart cherries can be substituted for frozen cherries.

CHERRY ANGEL DESSERT

1 package (6 ounces) cherry flavored gelatin
1 cup cold water
1 can (21 ounces) cherry filling and topping
1 can (8 ounces) pineapple tidbits, drained
1/2 of an angel food cake (store bought or homemade), cut into bite-size pieces
1 package (3.4 ounces) instant vanilla pudding
2 1/2 cups milk
1 container (8 ounces) frozen whipped topping, thawed
1/4 cup chopped pecans

In a large mixing bowl, combine gelatin and boiling water; stir until gelatin is dissolved. Add cold water. Let cool in refrigerator until gelatin is partly set, stirring occasionally. When gelatin is partly set, fold in cherry filling, pineapple and cake. Pour into an ungreased 13 x 9 x 2 inch baking pan. Spread gelatin mixture evenly over bottom of the pan. Prepare pudding according to package directions using 2 1/2 cups milk. Pour pudding over gelatin layer. Top with whipped topping; sprinkle with pecans. Refrigerate 2 to 3 hours, or overnight, before serving.

Makes 12 servings.

CHERRY MOCHA MOUSSE PIE

3 cups chocolate wafer crumbs
1/3 cup margarine, melted
1 can (21 ounces) cherry filling and topping, divided
1/4 cup granulated sugar
1 envelope unflavored gelatin
1 cup cold water
3 squares (1 ounce each) white baking bar with cocoa butter, chopped
3 egg yolks
1 1/2 cups heavy cream
2 tablespoons coffee liqueur
1 can (21 ounces) cherry filling and topping, divided
Chocolate curls or leaves for garnish

Lightly butter the bottom and sides of a 10-inch plate. in a mixing bowl, combine wafer crumbs and melted margarine. Press mixture firmly against the bottom and sides of prepared pan. Bake in a preheated 350 degree oven 8 minutes. When cool, spread 1/2 cup cherry pie filling evenly over crust; let chill. Cover remaining cherry filling and store in the refrigerator until serving time.

In a medium saucepan, combine sugar and gelatin; mix well. Add water and baking bar. Cook over medium heat, stirring constantly, until mixture boils and gelatin is dissolved. Put egg yolks in a mixing bowl; beat well. Add 1 cup hot gelatin mixture to yolks; stir until combined. Return all to saucepan. Cook over medium heat, stirring constantly, until mixture bubbles. Transfer gelatin mixture to a large mixing bowl. Let chill, stirring occasionally, 45 minutes, or until the consistency of unbeaten egg whites.

Meanwhile in a chilled mixing bowl with an electric mixer, beat cream until stiff peaks form. Add liqueur. Gently fold whipped cream mixture into gelatin mixture. Pour gelatin mixture into cooled pie crust. Let chill, covered overnight. Just before serving, spoon remaining cherry filling evenly over gelatin mixture. Garnish with additional whipped cream and chocolate curls or leaves. Makes 8 to 10 servings.

> *There are two types of cherries, sweet and tart. Sweet cherries are the larger, usually heart-shaped, firm and tender. Tart cherries are rounder and have a softer texture.*

SANTA'S CHERRY RING

The cherries and lemonade make a
salad that isn't too sweet.

10-ounce package red cherries, thawed
2 (3-ounce) package cherry flavored gelatin
2 cups boiling water
1 pint vanilla or cherry ice cream
1 (six-ounce) can frozen lemonade (3/4 cup)
1/4 cup pecans

Drain cherries, reserving syrup. Dissolve gelatin in boiling water. Add ice cream by
spoonsful, stirring until melted. Stir in lemonade concentrate and reserve syrup.
Chill until partially set. Add cherries and pecans. Turn into a six cup ring mold.
Chill until firm.

Makes 8 - 10 servings.

JEWISH COFFEE CAKE

Cake:
1 cup margarine
2 cups granulated sugar
6 eggs
1 teaspoon vanilla
1 tablespoon lemon juice
2 cups sour cream
4 cups all-purpose flour
1 teaspoon baking soda
1 1/2 teaspoons baking powder
1/2 teaspoon salt

Filling:
1 cup chopped walnuts
1/2 firmly packed brown sugar
1 teaspoon ground cinnamon
2 jars (10 ounces each) maraschino
cherries, cut into quarters

For the cake: In a large mixing bowl, combine margarine and sugar. Beat with an
electric mixer on medium speed until light and fluffy. Add eggs one at a time,
beating after each addition. Add vanilla and lemon juice; mix well. Combine flour,
baking powder, baking soda and salt. Add flour mixture and sour cream alternately
to sugar mixture.

For the filling: Combine walnuts, brown sugar and cinnamon. Starting with batter,
alternate batter, filling, and cherries in a greased and floured bundt pan, end with
sugar mixture and cherries. Bake in preheated 350 degree oven 1 hour, until done.

Makes 12 to 14 servings.

FRUIT FLUFF

1/2 pound or 32 - 34 marshmallows or 4 cups miniature marshmallows 1 cup milk.

Melt marshmallows with milk in the top of a double boiler.

1 1/4 cup flour
1/2 cup brown sugar
1/4 teaspoon salt
1/4 cup butter

Combine flour, sugar and salt. Cut in butter until fine. Place mixture in a 13 x 9 inch pan. Bake at 400 degrees for 10 - 12 minutes, stirring once. Take our 1/2 cup and save for topping. Press remainder in bottom of pan.

1 cup whipping cream or 1 package of Dream Whip with almond extract.
1 can cherry pie filling
almond extract

Beat whipping cream or Dream Whip with almond extract . Fold cool marshmallow mixture into whipped cream, turn 2/3 mixture into pan, spread to cover crumb layer. Spoon cherry filling over marshmallow layer and top with remaining marshmallow mixture. Sprinkle crumbs over top and chill over night.

Michigan is one of the leading cherry producing states, especially of tart cherries, producing 70-75% of all grown.

CHOCOLATE CHERRY TERRINE

Chocolate layer:
1/2 pound butter
1 1/3 pounds chocolate
4 ounces cocoa powder
9 eggs separated
3/4 cup sugar
1 cup heavy cream
2 tablespoons kirsch

Cherry layer:
1 1/2 cup individually quick frozen tart cherries, thawed
1/4 cup granulated sugar
4 tablespoons kirsch, divided
1 tablespoon lemon juice
1 1/2 teaspoons unflavored gelatin
2 tablespoons cherry preserves
1 cup heavy cream

For the chocolate layer: Melt chocolate and butter over a hot water bath; sift in cocoa. Let cool to room temperature.

In a large mixing bowl; combine egg yolks and sugar. Beat with an electric mixer on medium speed to ribbon stage. Fold into chocolate mixture. Be sure chocolate is not hot.

Beat egg whites to the soft peak stage. Gently fold whites into chocolate mixture.

For the cherry layer: In a medium saucepan, combine cherries, sugar, 2 tablespoons kirsch and lemon juice. Bring to a boil. Cover and boil 1 minute. Strain cherry mixture, reserve juices. Measure juices and pour into a saucepan. Boil until reduced to 1/4 cup; let cool. Sprinkle gelatin over reduced cherry juices. Let stand 10 minutes to soften. Cook over very low heat until gelatin dissolves. Add cherries, preserves and remaining mixture into a bowl. Set bowl over larger bowl filled with ice and water. Let stand 15 minutes, or until it begins to thicken but is not set, stirring frequently.

Beat cream in medium bowl to stiff peaks. Fold cream into cherry mixture.

To assemble terrine: This makes enough for 3 pans. For each pan, pour chocolate mixture halfway up a plastic lined terrine pan or regular bread pan. make a deep trough down the center and spoon the cherry filling into the trough. Smooth until trough is even with chocolate mixture, but do not mix into the chocolate. Fill the rest of the pan with chocolate mixture. Freeze overnight.

Makes 54 servings.

CHERRY MELTING MOMENTS COOKIES

1/2 cup sweet butter, softened
3 tablespoons confectioners' sugar
3/4 cup flour
1 teaspoon vanilla
Candied cherries

Preheat oven to 375 degrees.

Thoroughly combine butter, confectioners' sugar, flour and vanilla. Drop from teaspoon onto ungreased cookie sheet. Bake for 8 - 10 minutes until toothpick inserted in center comes out clean (test before 10 minutes). Place a candied cherry on top of each cookie immediately after they come out of oven.

CHERRY-PECAN COOKIES

Cookies:
3/4 cup solid vegetable shortening
1 1/2 cups granulated sugar
3 eggs
1 1/2 teaspoons vanilla
3 3/4 cups all-purpose flour
1/2 teaspoon baking soda
3/4 teaspoon salt

Filling:
2 cups dried tart cherries
1 cup granulated sugar
1 cup water
3/4 cup chopped pecans

For cookies: In a large mixing bowl, combine shortening, sugar and eggs. Beat with an electric mixer on medium speed until thoroughly combined. Stir in vanilla. Combine flour, baking soda and salt. Add flour mixture to batter; mix well. Let dough chill about 2 hours.

For the Filling: Using a food processor with the chopping blade, chop dried cherries. Place cherries in saucepan with sugar and water. Cook over medium heat, stirring constantly, until thickened (some remaining liquid is OK). Add pecans. Let cool.

To assemble cookies: On liberally floured board, roll 1/3 of dough as thin as possible (1/8 inch or less). Cut with a 2 1/2 inch cookie cutter. (Place scraps of dough to one side. Roll out when all other dough has been used up so that scraps are only reworked once.) Place on a greased baking sheet. Pile a heaping teaspoon of filling in center of each cookie. Cover with second cookie. Press lightly to distribute the filling and to get cookie tops and bottoms to match in shape. Press edges together lightly with fingertips.

Bake in a preheated 400 degree oven 8 to 10 minutes, or until slightly browned around the edges. Let cool on racks. Makes 3 1/2 dozen cookies.

FROZEN CHERRY CORDIAL PIE

1 1/2 cups chocolate wafers, crushed
6 tablespoons butter
10 ounces German chocolate, melted
1 (7 ounce) jar of marshmallow cream
1/3 cup cherry brandy
1/2 cup maraschino cherries, halved
2 1/2 cups whipping cream
6 whole cherries

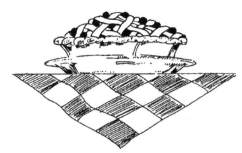

Combine crushed wafers and melted butter. Press into pie pan. Spread a thin layer of melted chocolate onto the bottom of the crust. Beat marshmallow cream and brandy. Fold in halved cherries. Beat 2 cups whipping cream. Fold in marshmallow cream. Turn into crust. Whip remaining cream and cherry juice. Use a pastry tube to pipe decorations around the top of the pie. Place the whole cherries and drizzle remaining melted chocolate on top of the pie. Freeze until solid. Serve and enjoy.

CHERRY COTTAGE PIE

2 tablespoons flour
1/2 cup sugar
1/8 teaspoon salt
2 eggs
2 cups cottage cheese
1/2 teaspoon vanilla
9" unbaked pie shell
1 (20 ounce) can cherry pie filling
Whipped cream (optional)

Put eggs and cottage cheese in blender. Blend until cottage cheese is pureed. Add sugar, salt, flour and vanilla and blend into cheese mixture. Pour into unbaked 9" pie shell. Bake at 350 degrees for 1 hour.

When cool, top with canned cherry pie filling. If desired, add whipped cream.

CHERRY CHEESE BARS

Crust:
1 cup walnuts, divided
1 1/4 cup unsifted all-purpose flour
1/2 cup firmly packed brown sugar
1/2 cup butter or oleo
1/2 cup flake coconut

Filling:
1 package (8 ounces) cream cheese, softened
1/3 cup granulated sugar
1 egg
1 teaspoon vanilla
1 can cherry pie filling

Preheat oven to 350 degrees. Grease bottom of a 9 x 13 inch pan. Chop 1/2 cup walnuts coarsely for topping; set aside. Chop remaining 1/2 cup of walnuts finely.

For crust: combine flour and brown sugar, cut in shortening until fine crumbs form. Add 1/2 cup finely chopped nuts and coconut. Remove 1/2 cup and set aside. Press remaining crumbs in pan; bake for 12 -15 minutes, or until edges are lightly browned.

For filling: beat cream cheese, sugar, egg and vanilla until smooth. Spread over hot baked crust; return to oven, bake 10 minutes longer. Spread cherry pie filling over cheese layer. Combine reserved coarsely chopped nuts and reserved crumbs. Sprinkle evenly over cherries. Bake 15 minutes longer. Cool. Cut into 24 squares.

CHERRY KEBABS

A colorful accompaniment for grilled or broiled chicken, fish or pork.

2 cups individually quick-frozen sweet cherries
2 cups pineapple chunks
1/4 cup red wine vinegar
2 tablespoons olive oil
1 tablespoon honey
1/2 teaspoon curry powder, or to taste

Partially thaw cherries, then thread them alternately with pineapple on bamboo skewers. In a small bowl, combine vinegar, oil, honey and curry powder; mix well. Place kebabs on broiler pan; broil 4 to 6 inches from heat. (Or grill over medium coals.) Brush with vinegar mixture. Cook 4 to 5 minutes, turning and basting with additional sauce after each turn. Makes 6 servings.

Note: Soak bamboo skewers in water to prevent burning during cooking. *Nutritional information per serving:*157 calories, 5 grams total fat, 0 mg cholesterol, 2 mg sodium.

DESSERT PIZZA

Better than pie and easier to prepare.

10 tablespoons light margarine, softened
1 3/4 cups all-purpose flour
1/3 cup confectioners' sugar
4 ounces Neufchatel cheese, softened
1/4 teaspoon ground cinnamon
1/4 teaspoon ground nutmeg
1 can (21 ounces) cherry filling and topping
1 medium apple or peach, cut into 18 slices
1 banana, sliced
1 can (8 ounces) pineapple chunks, drained and cut into bite size pieces.

In a mixing bowl with an electric mixer, beat margarine until light and fluffy. Add flour and confectioners' sugar. Continue beating until stiff dough forms.

Press dough onto a 12-inch pizza pan that has been coated with not-stick spray. Bake in a preheated 425-degree oven 8 to 10 minutes, or until golden brown. Let cool.

In a small mixing bowl, combine Neufchatel cheese, cinnamon and nutmeg; mix until smooth. Spread over cooled crust.

Remove 15 whole cherries from cherry filling; set aside. Put remainder of filling in electric blender of food processor; process until smooth. Pour puréed cherry filling evenly over cheese mixture.

Arrange apple or peach slices and bananas in a decorative pattern over cherry filling. Add pineapple pieces and reserved whole cherries to make an attractive presentation. Refrigerate until ready to serve. This dessert is best served within 1 to 2 hours after preparation.

Makes 12 servings.

Note: *Nutritional information per serving:* 246 calories, 9 grams total fat, 7 mg cholesterol, 137 sodium.

CHERRY-FILLED YELLOW CAKE

2/3 cup margarine or butter
1 3/4 cups sugar
2 eggs
1 1/2 teaspoons almond extract
3 cups cake flour
2 1/2 teaspoons baking powder
1 teaspoon salt
1 1/4 cups milk

Cream butter and sugar until light. Add eggs and almond extract; beat until fluffy. In another bowl, sift dry ingredients together. Add to creamed mixture alternately with milk, beating after each addition. Beat batter one more minute. Pour into greased 9 x 13 inch pan.

Filling:
2 cups frozen tart cherries, thawed
3/4 cup sugar
1/2 cup water
1 teaspoon almond extract
3 tablespoons cornstarch
1/4 cup water

Cook first four ingredients until boiling. Mix cornstarch and 1/4 cup water together. Add cornstarch mixture to cherries, cook until clear and thickened, stir constantly. Pour over cake batter, whirl into batter. Bake at 325 degrees, 1 hour.

CHERRY PHYLLO PIE

10 frozen phyllo leaves, thawed
1 1/2 cup butter, melted
1 cup sugar
3 tablespoons cornstarch
1 teaspoon lemon juice
2 (16 ounce) cans red tart cherries, drained

Preheat oven to 350 degrees. Trim stack of phyllo leaves into a 12 inch square; cover with damp towels. Separate 1 leaf and brush with butter. Place in ungreased, 9-inch pie plate, allowing corners to hang over edge of pie plate. Repeat with 4 more leaves. Mix sugar and cornstarch. Stir in lemon juice and cherries. Spread in phyllo-lined pie plate. Fold overhanging corners of phyllo over filling; spread each remaining phyllo leaf with butter. Arrange on filling to make top crust, allowing edges to hang over edge of plate. Fold over-hanging corners of phyllo under, between bottom layers and rim of plate. Cut through top layers of phyllo with scissors to make 8 sections. Bake until crust is golden and juice bubbles through cuts, about 45 minutes. Makes 8 servings.

CHERRY CRUMB PIE

Pastry: 3 8 inch, single crust pies
3 cups flour
1/2 cup (1 stick) margarine
1 cup shortening
1/4 teaspoon salt
1/2 cup ice water

Mix together flour, margarine, shortening and salt. Add ice water until thoroughly blended. Divide into 3 equal balls. (Sprinkle with a little flour for easier handling.) Refrigerate overnight. On a lightly floured surface, roll out each ball 2 inches larger than pie pan. Fit rolled pastry into pie pans; trim and flute edges. Bake or freeze 2 for later use.

Filling: (1 pie)
1 (21 ounce) can cherry pie filling
1/2 cup sugar
1/8 teaspoon cinnamon

Mix cherry pie filling, sugar and cinnamon. Pour into pastry-lined pie plate.

Topping: (1 pie)
1/2 cup sugar
3/4 cup flour
1/3 cup margarine

Mix sugar with flour. Cut in margarine until crumbly. Sprinkle over cherry filling.

Bake 45 to 50 minutes at 375 degrees.

To make sure that your baking powder is fresh, try pouring very hot tap water over a teaspoonful. If its fresh it will bubble very actively.

If cherry cookies are not browning properly, try placing them on a higher shelf.

To eliminate soggy pie shells, spread a thin layer of butter on the pie plate bottom before putting the dough in.

Butter your knife before you cut a pie with a soft filling.

CHERRY OATS SNACK CAKE

1 cup butter
1 cup firmly packed brown sugar
2 eggs
1 1/2 cups old fashioned or quick cooking rolled oats, uncooked
1/2 cup flour
1 teaspoon vanilla
1 cup dried cherries
1 (12 ounce) package chocolate chips, divided
Additional dried cherries for decorating

Using an electric mixer, cream butter and sugar in a large bowl. Add eggs; beat well. Add oats and flour; mix well. Stir in vanilla, cherries and 1 cup chocolate chips. Spread batter in ungreased 8 x 8 x 2 inch microwave-safe dish. Cover with waxed paper. Microwave on high 4 minutes and rotate dish 1/4 turn. Microwave on high 4 - 5 minutes longer until top of cake appears dry. Sprinkle remaining 1 cup chocolate chips over top of warm cake. Let stand 10 minutes to soften, then spread chocolate over cake. Sprinkle with additional dried cherries. Let cool completely before cutting.

BLACK FOREST CHERRY TORTE

Cherry Filling:
1/2 cup sifted confectioners' sugar
1/4 cup cherry flavored brandy
2 cups washed, pitted sweet cherries (1 pound)
1 1/2 tablespoons cornstarch

Combine confectioners' sugar and brandy. Stir well. Pour over cherries; toss gently and let stand two hours. Drain cherry liquid into medium sauce pan; add cornstarch and stir will. Add cherries; place over medium heat, and cook, stirring constantly until mixture begins to thicken. Boil 1 minute. Remove from heat. Cool, stirring occasionally. Yield: 2 cups.

Frosting:
1/2 cup butter or margarine, softened
2 cups sifted confectioners sugar
milk

Cream butter; gradually add confectioners' sugar, beating at a medium speed on an electric mixer. Add milk, one tablespoon at a time until spreading consistency. Beat until light and fluffy.

Assembly:
1 8-ounce commercial angel food loaf cake
frosting

cherry filling
1 ounce square semi-sweet chocolate, grated

Slice cake horizontally into 2 layers. Place one cake layer on serving platter; spread top and sides with frosting. Top evenly with cherry filling. Place remaining half cake over cherries. Spread top and sides with frosting. Dollop frosting around top and edge and base of torte. Sprinkle top of torte with grated chocolate.

Refrigerate until ready to serve.

Makes 6 to 8 servings.

BLACK CHERRY CUSTARD TART

Crust:
1 1/4 cups flour
1 tablespoon dark brown sugar
1/4 teaspoon salt
1/2 cup (1 stick) chilled, unsalted butter, cut in pieces
2 tablespoons cold water

Mix first three ingredients in food processor. Add butter and process using on/off turns until mixture resembles coarse corn meal. Add water and process until mixture forms large, moist clumps. Gather dough into ball. Flatten into disk. Wrap in plastic and refrigerate until well chilled, about 30 minutes. On lightly floured surface, roll dough to 11 inches in diameter. Roll up dough on a rolling pin and transfer to a 9 inch tart pan with removable bottom. Gently press into place. Trim edges. Freeze until firm (about 30 minutes).

Filling:
2 cups sweet Bing cherries, washed and pitted
4 tablespoons sugar, divided
3 egg yolks
1 tablespoon flour
2/3 cup whipping cream
1 tablespoon brandy
1/2 teaspoon vanilla extract
confectioners' sugar

Position rack in lowest 3rd of oven; preheat to 425 degrees. Bake crust until golden, about 15 minutes. Reduce oven temperature to 375 degrees. Remove from oven. Spread cherries evenly over bottom of shell. Sprinkle with 1 tablespoon sugar. Bake until cherries begin to soften, about 15 minutes. Remove from oven. In a small bowl, whisk remaining 3 tablespoons sugar with egg yolks and flour until smooth. Stir in whipping cream, brandy, and vanilla extract. Pour cream mixture over cherries. Return to oven and continue baking until custard sets, about 30 minutes. Cool slightly, 15-20 minutes. Release from pan, dust with confectioners' sugar.

CHERRY PIE

Pastry: for a two crust, 9 inch pie
2 cups flour
1 teaspoon salt 2/3 shortening
5 - 6 tablespoons water

Measure flour and salt into bowl. Cut in shortening thoroughly. Sprinkle with water. Stir lightly with fork until flour is moist and almost cleans sides of bowl. Gather dough into a ball, then divide in half. On a lightly floured surface, roll each half of dough 2 inches larger than pie pan. Fit one rolled pastry into 9 inch pie pan and set the other aside for top crust.

Filling:
1 1/3 cups sugar
1/3 cup flour
4 cups fresh red tart cherries, washed and pitted
3 tablespoons tapioca
1/4 teaspoon almond extract
2 tablespoons butter or margarine

Mix all ingredients, except butter in bowl. Pour into pastry lined pie pan. Dot with butter. Cover with top crust; trim and seal edges and cut vent slits. Bake at 425 degrees, 35 to 45 minutes. If necessary to prevent excessive browning, cover edges of crust with aluminum foil.

CHERRY PIE II

Filling:
3 cups frozen cherries
3 tablespoons cornstarch
1/4 teaspoon salt
1 cup sugar
1 tablespoon butter or margarine
1 or 2 drops of almond flavoring
1 or 2 drops of lemon flavoring
Few drops red food coloring

Crust:
2 cups flour
1 teaspoon salt
1/2 teaspoon baking powder
3/4 cup shortening
4 to 5 tablespoons milk

Filling:
Drain cherries, reserving juice, add water if needed to make 1 1/2 cups liquid. In saucepan, mix cornstarch with a little cherry juice to make a paste. Add rest of cherry juice and mix well. Stir in butter, flavorings and coloring. Fold in cherries. Cool while preparing crust.

Crust:
Sift flour, salt and baking powder into bowl. Cut in shortening. Sprinkle in milk, a tablespoon at a time, until all flour is moistened and dough cleans sides of bowl.

Form into a ball, divide in half and shape into flattened rounds on lightly floured board. Roll dough 2 inches larger than 9-inch pie pan. Fold pastry into quarters; unfold and ease onto pan. Pour cherry filling into pastry-lined pan. Cover edges with aluminum foil to prevent excessive browning. Bake at 425 degrees for 35 to 45 minutes.

CHERRY PIE III

4 cups frozen tart cherries, drained and thawed
1 cup sugar
3 tablespoons quick cooking tapioca
1/4 teaspoon red food coloring
1 teaspoon lemon juice
1/4 teaspoon almond extract
1 tablespoon butter or margarine, melted
Pastry for 2 crust 9-inch pie

Combine all ingredients except pastry; let stand about 15 minutes. Pour cherry mixture into unbaked pastry shell. Cover with top crust. Bake at 400 degrees for 55 minutes, or until well-browned.

CHERRY CROWNS

1 cup butter or margarine
1 cup sugar
1 egg yolk, lightly beaten
1 teaspoon almond extract
2 1/2 cups flour

1 egg white, lightly beaten
1/2 cup ground unblanched almonds
Candied cherries, halved

Cream butter and sugar. Add egg yolk and almond extract; mix well. Stir in flour. Chill dough one hour. Form dough into 1-inch balls, dip tops in lightly beaten egg white, then in ground almonds. Put on ungreased cookie sheet 2 inches apart.

Bake at 350 degrees about 15 minutes.

Press half a candied cherry, round side up into center of each cookie. Press gently to avoid shattering cookie. Remove from cookie sheet to cooling rack.

Makes about 4 1/2 dozen. Freezes well.

CHERRY COOL

1 can (16 ounces) sweet cherries
1/2 teaspoon almond extract
1 tablespoon grated orange peel
2 cups heavy cream

In an electric blender container, combine
cherries with liquid from the can, almond
extract and orange peel. Blend until smooth.

In a large, chilled mixing bowl, beat heavy cream until stiff
peaks form. Fold cherry mixture into whipped cream.
Spoon into parfait glasses. Let chill until ready to serve.
Makes 4 servings.

DRIED CHERRY STICKY CINNAMON ROLLS

Dough:
6 1/2 cups flour, divided
6 tablespoons sugar
2 packets yeast
1 1/2 teaspoons salt
1 cup milk
3/4 cup water
1/3 cup margarine
3 eggs

Mix 2 cups flour, sugar, and dry yeast. Heat milk, water and margarine to 120 - 130
degrees. Add to dry ingredients. Beat 2 minutes with electric mixer at medium
speed. Add eggs, one at a time, and 1/2 cup flour. Beat at high speed for 2 minutes.
Add enough remaining flour until dough clings to dough hook. Knead 8 to 10
minutes. Set in greased bowl and grease top of dough. Cover and let rise until
double, about 1 hour.

Syrup:
1 cup light corn syrup or maple syrup
2/3 cup packed brown sugar
6 tablespoons butter, melted
2 tablespoons water

Combine all ingredients in saucepan. Cook and stir over medium heat until brown
sugar is dissolved. Do not boil! Spread in 9 x 13 x 2 inch pan.

Assemble:
Butter, softened
Sugar
Cinnamon
Dried cherries
Chopped almonds - optional

Roll dough into long rectangle. Spread with soft butter. Sprinkle with sugar and cinnamon, a generous amount of dried cherries, and nuts. Roll up from long side. Cut into 1 1/2 inch pieces and place over syrup in pan. Let rise until double, about 1 hour.

Preheat oven to 375 degrees and bake for 30 minutes. Remove from oven and turn out onto serving platter. Cool.

CHERRY CHEESE TORTE

2 cups all-purpose flour
1/3 cup firmly packed brown sugar
1 cup chopped walnuts
1 cup margarine, softened
1 package (8 ounces) cream cheese, softened
1 cup confectioner's sugar
1 teaspoon vanilla
4 cups whipped topping
1 can (21 ounces) cherry filling and topping
Chopped walnuts or graham cracker crumbs (optional)

In a large mixing bowl, combine flour, brown sugar and walnuts. Cut in margarine until mixture is crumbly. Press flour mixture into an ungreased 13 x 9 x 2-inch baking pan. Bake in a preheated 375 degree oven 15 minutes. Remove from oven; break up crust with a fork. Repress into pan with a spatula while mixture is still warm. Let cool in the refrigerator.

In a large mixing bowl, combine cream cheese, confectioner's sugar and vanilla. Mix until smooth. Gently fold whipped topping into cream cheese mixture. Spread evenly over crust. Top with cherry filling. Sprinkle with chopped walnuts or graham cracker crumbs, if desired. Let chill in refrigerator 8 hours, or overnight.

Makes 12 to 15 servings.

CHERRY CAKE

1 1/2 cups granulated sugar
1 cup butter or margarine
1 tablespoon vanilla
4 eggs
2 cups sifted all-purpose flour
1 can (21 ounces) cherry filling and topping
Confectioner's sugar

In a mixing bowl with an electric mixer, beat sugar and butter until light and fluffy. Add vanilla; mix well. Add eggs, 2 at a time, beating well after each addition. Gradually add flour; beat well. Spread batter evenly in a greased and floured 15 x 10 x 1-inch baking pan.

Using a knife, lightly mark batter into 20 squares. Put a heaping tablespoon of cherry filling in the center of each square. Bake in a preheated 350 degree oven 30 to 50 minutes, or until lightly brown. Sprinkle with confectioner's sugar before serving.

Make 20 servings.

CHOCOLATE TEA COOKIES

6 ounces semi-sweet chocolate bits
1/4 cup milk
3/4 cup butter or margarine, softened
1/4 cup sugar
1 tablespoon maraschino cherry juice
1 1/2 cups flour
1/4 teaspoon salt
1/2 cup chopped maraschino cherries
1 cup rolled oats

Melt chocolate in milk over hot water. Cream butter; gradually add sugar and cherry juice. Sift together flour and salt. Add to creamed mixture. Stir in cherries, oats, and melted chocolate. Drop by teaspoons onto ungreased cookie sheets. Bake at 350 degrees for 12 to 15 minutes.

Makes about 3 1/2 dozen cookies.

CHERRY PUDDING CAKE

Cake:
1 cup granulated sugar
1/2 cup butter
2 eggs
1/2 cup milk
1 1/2 cups all-purpose flour
2 teaspoons baking powder
1/2 teaspoon salt
1/2 teaspoon ground nutmeg
1 can (16 ounces) pitted, tart cherries

Sauce:
Water
1 cup granulated sugar
1 tablespoon cornstarch
1 tablespoon butter
Salt, to taste
Ground nutmeg, to taste

Wow, More Facts...

Soft cherry cookies should be stored in a well sealed cookie jar with half an apple or a slice of bread. Change the apple or bread every 2 days.

When using plastic cookie cutters, they should be dipped in warm vegetable oil while you are working. You will get a cleaner, more defined edge on the patterns.

For cake: In a large mixing bowl with an electric mixer, beat sugar and butter until fluffy. Add eggs and milk; mix well. Combine flour, baking powder, salt and nutmeg. Add to sugar mixture. Drain cherries, reserving liquid. Fold drained cherries into batter. Pour batter into a greased 8 x 8 x 2-inch baking pan. Bake in a preheated 350 degree oven 45 to 50 minutes or until done.

For sauce: Add enough water to cherry liquid to make 2 cups; pour into a medium saucepan. Add sugar and cornstarch; mix until well combined. Add butter. Cook over high heat until mixture thickens and bubbles. Serve warm over cake.

Makes 6 to 8 servings.

And More Facts...

When making cherry frosting, try using a pinch of baking soda in the powdered sugar and the frosting won't crumble and dry as quickly.

To keep juices inside the crust when baking cherry pies with juicy fillings, try adding a teaspoon of tapioca before baking.

CHERRY BUTTER

40 pounds fresh sweet cherries
7 cups granulated sugar
1 tablespoon almond extract
1/2 teaspoon allspice, or more to taste

Rinse, drain and pit cherries. Purée in batches in an electric blender or food processor. You should have about 16 cups puréed cherries. In a large roasting pan or other large oven-proof container, combine puréed cherries, sugar, almond extract and allspice. Bake in a 300 degree oven 4 to 6 hours, stirring every 15 to 20 minutes. (The length of cooking depends on how juicy the cherries are. Cook until mixture is about half the original amount.)

While cherry mixture is cooking, clean and sterilize 6 to 7 pint canning jars. Pour hot cherry butter into jars. Seal with lids and rings. Process in a boiling water bath 10 minutes. Cool. Test seal. Store unopened containers at room temperature; store opened containers in the refrigerator. Use cherry butter as an appetizer with crackers or as a spread for bread.

Makes 6 to 7 pints.

24-CARAT CHERRIES AND ALMONDS

Golden glazed almonds glisten with cherries.

1 teaspoon ground cinnamon
1/4 teaspoon ground allspice
Dash of cayenne pepper
3/4 cups slivered almonds
1/2 cup dried tart cherries
1/4 cup granulated sugar
2 tablespoons butter or margarine

Line a baking sheet with aluminum foil; grease foil. Set aside. In a small bowl, combine cinnamon, allspice and cayenne; set aside.

In a large skillet, combine almonds, cherries, sugar and butter. Cook, stirring, over medium heat 10 minutes, or until sugar melts and turns a rich brown color. Be careful; mixture is hot! Remove from heat. Immediately stir in spice mixture. Quickly spread almond mixture on prepared pan. Let cool completely. Break into small clusters. Store in tightly covered container.

Makes about 1 1/2 cups.
Serving size: 1/4 cup, 195 calories per serving. Total fat per serving: 13 grams.

CHERRY BLOSSOMS

Prepared the night before, breakfast rolls have never been easier.

2/3 cup sifted confectioner's sugar
1/4 cup milk
1 cup dried tart cherries, divided
1/4 cup coarsely chopped pecans
1 loaf (14 to 16 ounces) frozen white bread dough, thawed
2 tablespoons butter or margarine, melted
1/4 cup brown sugar
1 1/2 teaspoons ground cinnamon

In a small mixing bowl, combine confectioner's sugar and milk; mix well. Pour mixture into a 9-inch deep-dish pie pan. Sprinkle 1/2 cup cherries and pecans evenly over sugar mixture.

On a lightly floured surface, roll bread dough into a 12 x 8-inch rectangle; brush with melted butter. In a small mixing bowl, combine brown sugar and cinnamon; sprinkle over dough. Top with remaining 1/2 cup cherries. Roll up rectangle, jelly-roll style, starting from a long side; pinch to seal edges. With a sharp knife, cut roll into 12 slices.

Place slices, cut-side down, on top of mixture in pan. Let rise, covered, in a warm place 30 minutes, or until nearly double. (Or, cover with waxed paper, then with plastic wrap.) Refrigerate 2 to 24 hours. Before baking, let chilled rolls stand, covered, 20 minutes at room temperature.

Bake, uncovered, in a preheated 375 degree oven 20 to 25 minutes for unchilled rolls and 25 to 30 minutes for chilled rolls, or until golden brown. If necessary, cover rolls with foil the last 10 minutes to prevent over-browning. Let cool in pan 1 to 2 minutes. Invert onto a serving platter. Serve warm.

Makes 12 rolls.

Serving size: 1 roll, 198 calories per serving. Total fat per serving: 6 grams.

CHERRY TIRAMISU

Easy version of an Italian classic.

1 cup Italian style ricotta cheese
1 cup confectioner's sugar
1/4 cup sour cream
1/4 cup coffee liqueur
1 1/2 cups shortbread cookie crumbs (about thirty 2-inch cookies)
1 can (21 ounces) cherry filling and topping
Grated chocolate, for garnish
Fresh mint leaves, for garnish

In a large mixing bowl, combine ricotta cheese, confectioner's sugar, sour cream and coffee liqueur; mix well. Set aside.

In an electric blender or food processor container, process cookies, in small batches, until finely crushed.

Remove 6 cherries from cherry filling; reserve for garnish.

To assemble dessert, spoon 2 tablespoons ricotta cheese mixture into each of six (8 ounce) parfait glasses. Add 2 tablespoons cookie crumbs to each glass; top each with 2 tablespoons cherry filling. Repeat ricotta, crumb and cherry filling. Repeat ricotta, crumb and cherry layers. Finish each serving with an equal portion of the remaining ricotta cheese mixture.

Garnish with reserved cherries, grated chocolate and mint leaves, if desired. Let chill 2 to 3 hours before serving.

Makes 6 servings.

Serving size: 1 (8 ounce) glass, 490 calories per serving. Total fat per serving: 14 1/2 grams.

CHERRY CASHEW COOKIES

Better than everyday chocolate chip cookies!

1 cup butter or margarine, softened
3/4 cup granulated sugar
3/4 cup firmly packed brown sugar
2 eggs
1 teaspoon vanilla extract
2 1/4 cups all-purpose flour
1 teaspoon baking soda
1 package (10 ounces) vanilla milk chips or
1 2/3 cups coarsely chopped white chocolate
1 1/2 cups dried tart cherries
1 cup lightly salted cashews

To avoid overbaking cookies, Just remove them from the oven a few minutes before they are done, the hot pan will continue to bake them.

Cherry sugar cookies will not get stiff or tough if you roll them out in sugar instead of flour.

In a large mixing bowl, combine butter, granulated sugar, brown sugar, eggs and vanilla. Mix with electric mixer on medium speed until thoroughly mixed. Combine flour and baking soda; gradually add flour mixture to butter mixture. Stir in vanilla milk chips, dried cherries and cashews. Drop by rounded tablespoonfuls onto ungreased baking sheets.

Bake in a preheated 375 degree oven 12 to 15 minutes, or until golden brown. Let cool on wire racks; store in a tightly covered container.

Makes 4 1/2 dozen cookies.

Serving size: 1 cookie, 126 calories per serving. Total fat per serving: 6 grams.

SUGARLESS CHERRY PIE

A pleasing alternative for special diets.

Replace 1 cup granulated sugar with an equivalent amount of dry sugar substitute.

Prepare pie as directed in star-spangled pie on page 112. Bake in a preheated 375 degree oven 50 to 55 minutes, or until juice begins to bubble through slits in crust.

Makes 8 servings.

Serving size: 1 wedge, calories per serving will vary. Total fat per serving: 16 1/2 grams.

STAR-SPANGLED PIE

An all-American tradition worth repeating.

4 cups frozen unsweetened tart cherries
1 cup granulated sugar
3 tablespoons quick-cooking tapioca
1/2 teaspoon almond extract
Pastry for 2-crust, 9-inch pie.
2 tablespoons butter or margarine

In a medium bowl, combine cherries,
granulated sugar, tapioca and almond
extract; mix well. (It is not necessary
to thaw cherries before using.) Let cherry
mixture stand 15 minutes.

Line a 9-inch pie plate with pastry; fill with
cherry mixture. Dot with butter. Adjust top
crust, cutting slits for steam to escape.

Bake in a preheated 400 degree oven 50 to
55 minutes, or until crust is golden brown
and filling is bubbly.

Makes 8 servings.

Note: 2 cans (16 ounces each) unsweetened tart cherries, well-drained, can be substituted for frozen tart cherries.

Serving size: 1 wedge, 399 calories per serving. Total fat per serving: 16 1/2 grams.

SUGARLESS CHERRY PIE II

3 cups frozen tart cherries
1 cup granulated artificial sweetener or its equivalent
1 tablespoon cornstarch
1/2 teaspoon almond extract
Pastry for two crust 8 inch pie

Combine ingredients except pastry; let stand 15 minutes. Pour into pastry-lined 8-inch pie pan. Cover with top crust. Bake at 400 degrees for 60 minutes.

Diabetic serving (1/6 of pie).

CHERRY CHOCOLATE BLOWOUT

Even the kids can help prepare this easy dessert.

1 package (21 1/2 ounces) brownie mix
1 can (21 ounces) cherry filling and topping
1/3 cup hot fudge topping, slightly warm
2 tablespoons chopped peanuts

Prepare brownie mix according to package directions. Divide batter between 2 greased 13 x 9 x 2-inch baking pans; spread batter evenly. Bake in a preheated 350 degree oven 15 to 20 minutes, or until brownies are done. Do not overbake. Let cool.

Cut one of the brownies into 1/2-inch cubes. Spread cherry filling evenly over remaining pan of brownies. Sprinkle brownie cubes over cherry filling. Drizzle fudge topping over brownie cubes. Sprinkle with peanuts. Cut into squares.

Makes 12 servings.

Serving size: 1 (3 inch) square, 334 calories per serving. Total fat per serving: 18 grams.

BLACK FOREST MOUSSE

This heavenly dessert is quick and convenient.

1 package (4 serving size) chocolate instant pudding and pie filling
2 cups cold milk
1 can (21 ounces) cherry filling and topping
2 cups frozen whipped topping, thawed

In a small bowl with an electric mixer, combine pudding mix and milk. Beat on low speed 1 to 2 minutes, or until well-blended. Allow pudding to thicken slightly, then stir in cherry filling. Gently fold in whipped topping.

Spoon into parfait glasses or other dessert dishes; let chill until serving time.

Makes 8 servings.

Serving size: 3/4 cup, 223 calories per serving. Total fat per serving: 6 1/2 grams.

CHERRY SUNDAE PIE

1 1/3 cups sifted flour
1/2 teaspoon salt
1/2 cup shortening
3 tablespoons water
1 1/2 pints softened vanilla ice cream
1 (21 ounce) can cherry pie filling, chilled

Combine flour and salt. Cut in shortening until uniform but coarse. Sprinkle with water, toss with a fork and shape into a ball. On a lightly floured board, roll out the pastry 1 1/2-inches larger than inverted 9-inch pie plate. Fit into plate; rim and flute. Prick sides and bottom with fork. Bake in 425 degree oven 20 to 25 minutes, or until browned. Cool. Scoop ice cream into cooled pie shell. Freeze until firm. To serve, spoon pie filling over ice cream.

RIBBON OF CHERRY CHEESECAKE

Swirls of cherry give cheesecake new dimension.

1 cup sliced almonds
1 cup graham cracker crumbs
1/3 cup butter or margarine, melted
1 can (21 ounces) cherry filling and topping
3/4 cup plus 2 tablespoons granulated sugar; divided
2 tablespoons cornstarch
1/2 teaspoon almond extract
4 packages (8 ounces each) cream cheese, softened
3 tablespoons Amaretto liqueur
1 tablespoon lemon juice
1 teaspoon vanilla extract
3 eggs, slightly beaten

In a skillet over medium heat, toast almonds. Remove from heat; finely chop almonds. In a medium bowl, combine almonds, graham cracker crumbs and butter; mix well. Press crumb mixture evenly 2 inches up the sides and over the bottom of a 10-inch spring-form pan. Set aside.

In an electric blender or food processor container, purée cherry filling until smooth. Pour puréed cherry filling into a medium saucepan. Combine 2 tablespoons granulated sugar and cornstarch; stir into cherry filling.

Cook, stirring constantly over low heat until mixture is thick and bubbly. Remove from heat. Stir in almond extract. Set aside to cool.

In a mixing bowl with an electric mixer, combine cream cheese, remaining 3/4 cup sugar, Amaretto, lemon juice and vanilla; beat until light and fluffy. Add eggs all at once, beating on low speed just until mixed. Do not overheat.

To assemble the cheesecake, pour one-third of the cream cheese mixture into prepared crust. Top with about 1/3 cup of the cherry purée. Swirl cherry mixture into cream cheese using a knife or spatula. Repeat layers twice, ending with cherry purée. Reserve remaining purée.

Bake in a preheated 350 degree oven 60 to 65 minutes or until the center appears nearly set when gently shaken. Do not let the top crack. Cool on a wire rack. Let chill. To serve, spoon a generous tablespoon of purée on serving plate. Place cheesecake wedge on top of purée.

Makes 16 servings.

Serving size: 1 wedge, 395 calories per serving. Total fat per serving: 28 grams.

POLKA DOT COOKIES

1/2 cup butter or margarine
1/4 cup granulated sugar
1/2 cup brown sugar, packed
1 egg, slightly beaten
1 teaspoon vanilla
2 cups flour
1 teaspoon baking powder

1/4 teaspoon baking soda
1/2 teaspoon salt
1/4 cup 1 % milk
6 ounces chocolate chips
1/2 cup chopped maraschino cherries
1/2 cup chopped nuts

Cream butter, granulated sugar and brown sugar. Blend in egg and vanilla. Sift together flour, baking powder, baking soda, and salt; add alternately with milk, mixing well after each addition. Stir in chocolate chips, cherries and nuts. Drop rounded teaspoonsful on greased baking sheet. Bake at 375 degrees for 10 - 12 minutes.

Makes about 3 1/2 dozen cookies.

When reusing a cookie pan for numerous batches try running the bottom of the pan under cold water, but don't get the top wet. This will reduce the chance of bottom burned cherry cookies.

The best way to cut a cherry angel food cake is with an electric knife.

Before baking a pie that is juicy, insert a tube of macaroni in the center of the top of the pie and the juices won't bubble out.

CHERRY CHIP PIE

3/4 cup sugar
2 tablespoons quick cooking tapioca
1/4 teaspoon salt
4 cups pitted fresh tart cherries
1/3 cup semi-sweet chocolate pieces
Pastry for a 9-inch lattice top pie

Combine sugar, tapioca and salt. Stir in cherries and chocolate pieces. Let stand 15 minutes. Use half the pastry to line 9-inch pie plate. Put cherry mixture into pastry-lined pie plate. Cut lattice strips from remaining pastry; lay lattice strips on filling; seal and flute edges. Bake at 375 degrees for 40 to 45 minutes or till done. Cover edges with foil, if necessary, to prevent overbrowning. Cool.

NO-BAKE CHERRY CHEESE SQUARES

Fluffy, light and just a hint of lemon.

1 1/4 cups graham cracker crumbs.
1/2 cup granulated sugar, divided
1/3 cup butter or margarine, melted
1 package (3 ounces) cream cheese, softened
2 teaspoons grated lemon peel
1 teaspoon vanilla extract
2 cups frozen whipped topping, thawed
1 can (21 ounces) cherry filling and topping
1/2 teaspoon almond extract

In a medium bowl, combine graham cracker crumbs, 1/4 cup sugar and melted butter; mix well. Press crumb mixture firmly into the bottom of a 9 x 9 x 2-inch baking pan. Let crust chill while preparing the rest of the ingredients.

In a mixing bowl with an electric mixer, combine cream cheese, remaining 1/4 cup sugar, lemon peel and vanilla; beat until light and fluffy. Fold in whipped topping. Pour into prepared crust.

Combine cherry filling and almond extract. Pour over cheese filling. Let chill until ready to serve.

Makes 9 servings.

Serving size: 1 (3 inch) square, 323 calories per serving. Total fat per serving: 16 grams.

CHERRY SUPREME

Dressing:
2 tablespoons sour cream
1 tablespoon salad dressing
1 teaspoon sugar
1/8 teaspoon salt

Salad:
2 cups dark sweet cherries
1 cup pineapple chunks
1 cup diced celery
1 (3 ounce) package Lite-cream
   cheese, diced
1/4 cup walnut meats, cut up

Dressing:
Mix well and chill

Salad:
Drain cherries well, set aside in refrigerator. Combine pineapple, celery and cheese; toss lightly. Make a bed of lettuce in serving bowl or individual salad plates. Arrange pineapple, celery, and cream cheese combination on the lettuce. Just before serving, arrange the cherries and walnut meats over the salad. Serve with the dressing over all. Do not stir.

FROZEN CHERRY DESSERT

1 (6 ounce) package Lite-cream cheese
1 cup salad dressing
1 cup whipping cream, whipped
3 1/2 cups drained crushed pineapple
1/2 cup maraschino cherries, red or green, halved
2 1/2 cups small marshmallows

Cream together cream cheese and salad dressing. Fold in other ingredients. Put in 9-inch square pan or loaf pan; freeze. For best results, leave in freezer until just before serving. To serve turn onto plate, slice or cut in squares, about 10 servings.

CHERRY RING

Salad:
4 teaspoons unflavored gelatin
1/4 cup cold water
1 (16 ounce) can tart cherries
1/2 cup sugar
1/3 cup grapefruit juice
1/8 teaspoon salt
1/4 teaspoon red food coloring

Cream Cheese Dressing:
3 ounces cream cheese, softened
1 tablespoon salad dressing
3 tablespoons thin cream
1/8 teaspoon salt
1 tablespoon chopped nuts

Salad:
Soften gelatin in cold water 5 minutes. Drain juice from cherries and heat to boiling. Add softened gelatin, and stir until dissolved. Stir in sugar. Add grapefruit juice, salt and red food coloring. Pour into oiled 3 cup mold. Refrigerate until set. Unmold onto chilled serving plate. Serve with cream cheese dressing.

Cream Cheese Dressing:
Blend together cream cheese, salad dressing, cream and salt until smooth. Fold in nuts.

TART CHERRY MOLD

1 (16 ounce) can tart cherries
1 (8 1/2 ounce) can crushed pineapple
1/2 cup sugar
1 (6 ounce) package cherry gelatin
1 1/2 cups ginger ale
1/2 cup chopped nuts optional
1/2 cup shredded coconut

Drain fruits, reserving juices. Add water to juices if needed to make 2 cups liquid. Bring liquid to a boil; stir in sugar and gelatin until dissolved. Cool. Add fruit and ginger ale. Chill until very thick but not set. Stir in nuts and coconut. Pour into an oiled quart mold. Chill until set.

BING CHERRY SUPREME

1 (16 ounce) can dark sweet cherries
1 cup crushed pineapple
1 cup mandarin orange sections
1 tablespoon unflavored gelatin
1 (3 ounce) package raspberry gelatin
1 cup pecans, chopped
1 cup cola
1/2 cup whipping cream, whipped
1 tablespoon Lite-mayonnaise

Drain fruits separately, reserving juices. Measure cherry juice and if necessary, add pineapple juice to make 1 cup liquid. Soften unflavored gelatin in 1/4 cup pineapple juice. Heat cherry juice; pour over raspberry gelatin. Add gelatin softened in pineapple juice; stir until dissolved. Pour into 1 1/2 quart mold. Chill until it thickens. Add fruits, nuts and cola. Combine whipped cream and mayonnaise. Fold into gelatin. Chill.

Makes about 8 - 10 servings.

BING CHERRY DESSERT

1 (16 ounce) can dark sweet cherries
3 ounce package cherry gelatin
1 cup cold water
1 (8 ounce) package cream cheese, softened
1/3 cup almonds, pecans or walnuts

Drain cherries, reserving juice; add water if needed to make 1 cup liquid. Boil cherry juice, dissolving gelatin in it. Add cold water. Cool. Cream cheese until soft. Stir into thickened gelatin. Fold in nuts and cherries. Pour into oiled 4 cup mold. Chill until firm.

DOUBLE CHERRY TURNOVERS

Sour cream pastry:
3 cups sifted flour
2 tablespoons sugar
1 cup butter or margarine
1 cup sour cream

Double cherry filling:
2 cups tart cherries, drained
3/4 cup cherry jam
1/4 cup chopped almonds
Almond flavoring, optional
red food coloring, optional

Sour Cream pastry:
Combine flour and sugar; cut in butter with a pastry blender until mixture is crumbly. Add sour cream; mix lightly with a fork until dough clings together with hands and knead a few times. Wrap dough in plastic wrap or waxed paper; chill several hours or overnight.

Double Cherry Filling:
Combine all ingredients, mix well. Roll out 1/2 dough to 15 x 10-inch rectangle; trim edges evenly with pastry wheel or sharp knife. Cut into six 5-inch squares. Put about 2 tablespoons filling on each square. Moisten edges with water; fold over to make triangles. Crimp edges with fork to seal. Make vent slits in top. Lift onto greased cookie sheet. Sprinkle with sugar. Preheat oven to 400 degrees then lower heat to 375 degrees and bake 25 minutes, or until puffed and rich brown; remove to wire rack to cool.

Makes 12 turnovers.

CHERRY CHIFFON PIE

1 (16 ounce) can tart cherries
1 envelope unflavored gelatin
2/3 cup sugar
3 egg whites
1/4 teaspoon cream of tartar
1/3 cup sugar
1/2 cup heavy cream,whipped
9-inch baked pastry shell

Drain cherries, reserving juice. Soften gelatin in juice. Heat cherries with 2/3 cup sugar to boiling. Add gelatin and stir until dissolved. Cool until mixture begins to thicken.

Beat egg whites and cream of tartar until fluffy. Gradually add 1/3 cup sugar and beat until stiff. Fold cherry mixture into egg whites. Fold in whipped cream. Pile into baked pastry shell. Chill several hours or overnight. Garnish as desired.

CHERRY-BERRY PIE

1 1/2 cups tart cherries
1 (10 ounce) package frozen red raspberries
3 tablespoon tapioca
1 cup sugar
Pastry for 2-crust 9-inch pie
1 tablespoon butter

Mix fruits; add tapioca combined with sugar; let stand 15 minutes. Pour into 9-inch pastry lined pie pan; dot with butter. Moisten edge of bottom crust, adjust top crust, seal to lower crust and flute edge. Bake at 450 degrees for 10 minutes. Reduce heat to 350 degrees and continue baking for about 30 minutes, until crust is brown and filling bubbles.

CHERRY CRESCENTS

4 ounces cream cheese, softened
1/2 cup butter or margarine, softened
1 cup flour
1/4 teaspoon salt
1/2 cup cherry preserves
1/2 cup chopped walnuts
2 teaspoons grated lemon peel
1 egg yolk
1 to 2 teaspoons milk

Cream together cream cheese and butter with a spoon. Gradually work in flour and salt until well-blended. Form into a ball. Chill for 1 hour in freezer 4 hours to overnight in refrigerator. Cut dough in half; on well floured pastry cloth, roll out each half into an 8 to 9-inch circle 1/8 inch thick. Trim to make circles perfectly round. Cut each circle into 16 wedges.

Combine preserves, nuts and lemon peel. Put about 1/2 teaspoon of mixture in center of wide edge of wedge. Roll up, starting with wide edge, shaping into a crescent.

Beat egg yolk slightly with milk; brush on pastry. Bake at 350 degrees for 15 to 20 minutes on upper shelf of oven, until slightly browned. Cool. Dust with powdered sugar, if desired.

CHERRY PIE SUPREME

1 (21 ounce) can cherry pie filling
1   9-inch unbaked pie shell
12 ounces cream cheese, softened
1/2 cup sugar
2 eggs
1/2 teaspoon vanilla extract
1 cup sour cream

Spread half of cherry pie filling in bottom of pie shell. Bake at 425 degrees for 15 minutes or just until crust is golden. Remove from oven. Reduce oven temperature to 350 degrees.

Cream cheese with sugar, eggs and vanilla until smooth. Pour over hot cherry pie filling; bake 25 minutes. (Filling will be slightly soft in center.) Cool completely on wire rack. To serve, spoon sour cream around edge of pie. Fill center with remaining cherry pie filling.

REFRIGERATOR CHEESE PIES

Crust:
1 1/2 cups graham cracker or zwieback
  crumbs
1/2 cup powdered sugar
6 tablespoons melted butter or margarine
1 teaspoon cinnamon, optional

Filling:
2 tablespoons unflavored gelatin
1/2 cup cold water
2 egg yolks, beaten
1/2 cup sugar
1/2 cup milk or cream
1 teaspoon salt
2 cups small curd cottage cheese
1 teaspoon grated lemon rind
3 tablespoon lemon juice
1 teaspoon vanilla
1 cup heavy cream, whipped
2 egg whites, stiffly beaten

Cherry Glaze:
1 (16 ounce) can tart cherries
1/3 cup sugar
1/16 teaspoon salt
2 tablespoons cornstarch
1 tablespoon butter or margarine
1/3 teaspoon grated lemon rind
1/8 teaspoon red food coloring

Crust:
Combine ingredients. Pat into two 9-inch pie pans. Cover sides and bottoms of pans. Chill thoroughly.

Filling:
Soak gelatin in cold water. In top of double boiler, cook egg yolks, sugar, milk and salt. When mixture begins to thicken stir in soaked gelatin until dissolved. Chill in pan of ice water. Beat until smooth. Stir in cottage cheese, lemon rind, lemon juice and vanilla. Fold in whipped cream. Fold in stiffly beaten egg whites. Fill pie shells. Chill 4 hours or longer.

Cherry Glaze:
Drain cherries, reserving juice. Mix sugar, salt and cornstarch. Add drained cherry juice. Cook, stirring constantly until thick and clear. Add butter, cherries, lemon rind and food coloring. Cool. Spoon over cheese filling.

If a pie shell blisters, try placing a few slices of white bread on the shell before baking. Then bake and remove the bread just before its finished.

ALMOND CRUST CHERRY CREAM PIE

Pie crust mix for single crust 9-inch pie
1/2 cup slivered almonds, finely chopped
1 (14 ounce) can sweetened condensed milk
1/3 cup lemon juice
1 teaspoon vanilla
1 teaspoon almond flavoring
1/2 cup whipping cream, whipped
1 (21 ounce) can cherry pie filling

Prepare pastry as directed on package, adding almonds. Line 9-inch pie plate. Bake at 425 degrees for 12 to 15 minutes. Cool.

Combine condensed milk, lemon juice, vanilla and almond flavoring. Fold in whipped cream. Spoon into cooled pie shell. Top with pie filling. Chill several hours before serving.

CHERRY BANANA PIE

1 (3 1/4 ounce) package vanilla pudding mix
2 cups milk
2 medium bananas
lemon juice
9-inch pie shell, baked
1 (21 ounce) can cherry pie filling
1 cup whipping cream
2 tablespoons sugar
1/3 cup chopped nuts

Prepare pudding with milk according to package directions; cool. Slice bananas; coat with lemon juice. Put in bottom of pie shell. Spread cooled pudding over bananas. Top with cherry pie filling. Whip cream, adding sugar gradually; spread over cherries. Sprinkle nuts over top.

CHOCOLATE CHERRY CREAM PIE

1 cup (10 ounce jar) sliced red maraschino cherries
2 cups chocolate pudding
9-inch pie crust, baked
2 cups whipped dessert topping

Fold cherries into pudding. Fill pie crust. Cover with whipped topping. Garnish with cherries, if desired.

FESTIVE CHERRY MERINGUE PIE

Meringue:

3 egg whites
1 teaspoon vanilla
1 cup sugar

3/4 cup chopped walnuts
1/2 cup finely crushed saltine crackers
1 teaspoon baking powder

Beat egg whites and vanilla until foamy. Gradually add sugar, beating until stiff peaks form. Mix together nuts, cracker crumbs and baking powder; fold into egg whites. Spread into well-greased 9-inch pie plate, building up sides. Bake at 300 degrees for about 40 minutes or until dry on outside; cool.

Filling:
1 (20 ounce) can (2 1/2 cups) frozen tart cherries, thawed and
drained, reserving liquid
1/4 cup sugar
1/4 teaspoon almond extract
2 tablespoons cornstarch
1 cup whipped cream

In saucepan, combine 3/4 cup of reserved cherry syrup, sugar and almond extract; heat to boiling. Add cherries; cook 5 minutes. Combine cornstarch and remaining cherry syrup; add to hot mixture in saucepan. Cook and stir until thickened and bubbly. Cool.

Line meringue shell with 3/4 of the whipped cream. Fill cooled cherry mixture. Garnish with dollops of whipped cream.

CHERRY CRUNCH CHIFFON PIE

Crust:
1 1/4 cups rolled oats
1/3 cup brown sugar
1/3 cup melted butter or margarine

Combine ingredients. Bake at 350 degrees for 10 minutes, stirring occasionally. Press onto sides and bottom of 9-inch pie plate. Cool before filling.

Filling:
1 (16 ounce) can tart cherries
1/3 cup sugar
1 envelope unflavored gelatin
3 egg yolks, slightly beaten
Red food coloring
1/3 cup sugar
3 egg whites, beaten until foamy
2 cups whipped dessert topping

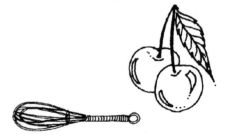

Drain cherries, reserving 2/3 cup juice. Combine 1/3 cup sugar and gelatin in saucepan; add cherry juice; bring to a boil. Add a little of this liquid to egg yolks, return to saucepan and cook over low heat 2 minutes, stirring constantly. Stir in cherries and coloring. Chill until mixture begins to set.

Gradually add 1/3 cup sugar to egg whites; beat to stiff peaks. Fold into cherry mixture. Fold in dessert topping. Pour into shell. Chill several hours before serving.

CHERRY-PECAN REFRIGERATED COOKIES

3/4 cups shortening
1 egg
1 teaspoon vanilla
1 cup brown sugar
2 cups sifted flour
1/2 teaspoon baking soda
1/2 teaspoon salt
1/2 teaspoon cream of tartar
1/4 cup maraschino cherries, finely chopped
1/2 cup chopped pecans

Cream shortening, egg, vanilla and brown sugar. Sift together flour, baking soda, salt and cream of tartar. Add half at a time to creamed mixture and beat will. Stir in cherries and nuts.

Divide dough in half; shape each half in a roll about 2 inches in diameter. Wrap in waxed paper and chill until firm. Cut into 1/8 inch slices. Bake on ungreased cookie sheet at 400 degrees for 6 - 8 minutes. Cool 1 to 2 minutes before removing from pan.

Makes about 5 dozen cookies.

CHERRY OATMEAL COOKIES

1 cup flour
3/4 teaspoon baking soda
1/2 teaspoon salt
3/4 cup soft shortening
1 1/3 cups firmly packed brown sugar
2 eggs
1 teaspoon vanilla
1/4 teaspoon almond extract
1 cup dried cherries, cut up
2 cups rolled oats

Sift together flour, baking soda and salt. Add shortening, sugar, eggs, vanilla and almond extract; beat until smooth, about 2 minutes. Stir in cherries and oatmeal. Drop by heaping teaspoonsful onto greased cookie sheets. Bake at 350 degrees for 12 to 15 minutes. Makes about 3 1/2 dozen cookies.

CHRISTMAS CHERRY COOKIES

1 cup butter or margarine
1/2 teaspoon vanilla extract
1 cup sifted confectioner's sugar
1/2 teaspoon almond extract
1/4 teaspoon salt
1 (8 ounce) jar maraschino cherries, drained and cut up
2 cups unsifted flour
1/2 cup chopped almonds

Cream butter; add sugar and cream again. Add salt, flour, vanilla extract and almond extract; add drained cherries and nuts. Chill. Shape into small balls. Bake on ungreased cookie sheet at 275 degrees for 30 to 35 minutes. While warm, dip in confectioner's sugar. Yield; 4 to 5 dozen.

CHERRY BOWTIES

2 1/2 cups flour
1 tablespoon sugar
1 teaspoon salt
1 cup shortening
1 egg yolk
Milk
3/4 cup cherry jam or preserves

Mix flour, sugar and salt. Cut in shortening. Mix egg yolk with enough milk to make 2/3 cup; add to dough and form into a ball. Roll out dough between 2 pieces of wax paper, to 1/8 inch thickness. Cut into 2 inch squares. Fill with 1 teaspoon cherry jam. Fold opposite corners to center and pinch together to resemble bow ties. Bake on ungreased cookie sheet at 400 degrees for about 10 minutes. Cool. Dust with powdered sugar. Makes about 3 dozen.

Simple Tips To Help You Out...

Wheat flour will give you crunchier cherry cookies if butter is used as the shortening. If oil is used the cookies will be more tender & moist.

When making pie dough, you may use lard instead of butter. The crust will come out flakier and lard actually has less saturated fat.

CHERRY MERINGUE BARS

1/2 cup butter or margarine
1/2 cup powdered sugar
1 cup flour
2 egg yolks
1 cup cherry jam or preserves

2 egg whites
1/2 cup sugar
1/2 cup slivered almonds, optional

Cream butter and sugar; blend in flour and egg yolks. With wet hands, spread mixture on bottom of a 9 x 13-inch pan. Bake at 350 degrees for 18 minutes. Cool. Spread cherry jam over crust.

Beat egg whites until fluffy; gradually add 1/2 cup sugar. Continue beating until stiff peaks form.

Top cherries with meringue. Sprinkle with slivered almonds. Bake at 350 degrees for 10 to 20 minutes or until meringue is golden brown.

FRUIT CRUNCH BARS

3/4 cup butter or margarine
1 cup brown sugar
1 3/4 cups flour
1 teaspoon salt
1/2 teaspoon baking soda
1 1/2 cups rolled oats
1 (21 ounce) cherry pie filling

Mix butter and brown sugar. Add flour, salt, baking soda and rolled oats. Mix until crumbly. Press 1/2 of mixture into 9 x 13-inch pan. Spread with can of cherry pie filling. Sprinkle with remaining crumb mixture. Bake at 400 degrees for 25 minutes. Cool and cut into bars.

More Simple Tips...

Before you place a cake on a plate, sprinkle the plate with sugar to prevent the bottom of the cake from sticking to the plate.

If you want to revive a stale cherry cake, just dip it quickly in cold low-fat milk and heat it in a 350 degree oven for 15 minutes or until soft.

CHERRY BAR COOKIES

1 cup dried cherries
1 cup chopped walnuts
1 cup packed brown sugar
3/4 cup flour

1 1/2 teaspoons baking powder
1/4 teaspoon salt
3 eggs, well-beaten

Combine cherries, walnuts, brown sugar, flour, baking powder and salt; mix. Fold into eggs. Spread in greased 9-inch square pan. Bake at 325 degrees for 25 - 30 minutes. Cool in pan 5 - 10 minutes. Cut into 24 pieces (1" x 3"). Roll in confectioner's sugar if desired.

CHERRY–DATE LOGS

3 eggs
1 cup sugar
1 1/2 cups flour
1 1/2 teaspoons baking powder
1 teaspoon vanilla

2 1/2 cups dates, cut up
1 cup dried cherries
1/2 cup nuts, chopped
1 teaspoon red food coloring

Beat eggs and sugar. Sift together flour and baking powder. Add vanilla to egg mixture. Fold in dates, cherries, nuts and coloring. Spread on a greased 10 x 15-inch jelly roll pan. Bake at 350 degrees for 30 to 40 minutes. Cut while hot in 1 x 4-inch pieces and roll in powdered sugar while warm.

DREAM BARS

1/2 cup soft butter or margarine
1/2 cup brown sugar, packed
1 cup flour
1 cup cherry jam or preserves
2 eggs, beaten

1 cup brown sugar, packed
2 tablespoons flour
1 teaspoon baking powder
1/2 teaspoon salt
1/2 teaspoon vanilla or almond
1 cup coconut
1 cup chopped nuts

Combine butter, 1/2 cup brown sugar and 1 cup flour. Pat into bottom of an ungreased 9 x 13-inch pan. Bake at 350 degrees for 10 minutes. Remove from oven and carefully spread with layer of cherry jam.

Combine eggs, 1 cup brown sugar, 2 tablespoons flour, baking powder, salt and vanilla; beat well. Stir in coconut and nuts. Spread over the jam layer. Bake at 350 degrees for 30 minutes. When cool, cut into squares or bars to serve.

CHERRY COCONUT BARS

Pastry:
1 cup flour
3 tablespoons powdered sugar
1/2 cup butter or margarine

Topping;
2 eggs, slightly beaten
1 cup sugar
1/4 cup flour
1/2 teaspoon baking powder
1/2 teaspoon salt
1 teaspoon vanilla
1 cup chopped nuts
1/2 cup coconut
1/2 cup chopped maraschino cherries

Pastry:
Combine ingredients until mixture resembles coarse cornmeal. Pat into bottom of an ungreased 9-inch square pan. Bake at 350 degrees for 25 minutes.

Topping:
Combine eggs, sugar, flour, baking powder, salt and vanilla; beat well. Stir in coconut, nuts and cherries. Spread over the baked pastry. Bake at 350 degrees for 25 minutes, or until lightly browned. When cool, cut into squares or bars to serve.

CHERRY BROWNIES

1/2 cup butter or margarine
1/2 teaspoon salt
2 ounces unsweetened chocolate
1/2 teaspoon vanilla
2 eggs
1/2 cup chopped and drained tart cherries
1 cup sugar
1 cup chopped nuts, optional
1 cup flour
1 teaspoon baking powder

Melt butter and chocolate together; cool. Beat eggs; add sugar and beat well. Sift flour, baking powder and salt together; add to egg and sugar mixture. Add cooled chocolate mixture and vanilla; mix well. Fold in cherries and nuts. Bake in greased 8-inch square pan for 45 minutes at 300 degrees.

BUTTERSCOTCH JEWEL BARS

Bottom Layer:
1/2 cup butter or margarine
1 cup dark brown sugar
1 egg
2 cups flour
1/4 teaspoon nutmeg
3/4 teaspoon salt
3 tablespoons milk
1/2 cup raisins, white or dark
1 1/2 cups broken pecans
3/4 cup candied red cherries, halved
2 eggs
1/4 cup sugar
1 teaspoon vanilla
1 teaspoon brandy or almond extract

Top Layer:
3/4 cup diced candied green pineapple or candied fruit

Bottom Layer:
Cream butter and brown sugar on high speed; add egg and beat on low speed. Sift flour, nutmeg and salt together. Add alternately with milk to butter mixture using low speed. Spread in a greased 15 1/2 x 10 1/2 x 1-inch jelly roll pan. Bake at 350 degrees for 10 minutes.

Top Layer:
Mix pineapple, raisins, pecans, and cherries. Beat eggs slightly and add sugar and flavorings using low speed; add to fruit mixture and mix well. Spread fruit mixture over hot bottom layer. Return to oven and bake at 350 degrees for 20 minutes. While still warm cut into 2 x 1 1/2 bars.

When baking a pie with a graham cracker crust, dip the pan in warm water for 10 seconds and it will be easier to remove in one piece.

Cherry angel food cake should be cooled by turning the pan upside down over a tray of ice cubes.

CHOCOLATE CHERRY BARS

Bars:
2 layer chocolate fudge cake mix
1 (21 ounce) can cherry pie filling
2 eggs, beaten
1 teaspoon almond extract

Frosting:
1 cup sugar
5 tablespoons butter or margarine
1/3 cup milk
6 ounces semi-sweet chocolate chips

Bars:
Combine ingredients; stir by hand until well mixed. Pour into greased and floured 15 x 10-inch jelly roll pan. Bake at 350 degrees for 25 to 30 minutes (or bake in 9 x 13-inch pan for 40 minutes). Cool.

Frosting:
In saucepan, combine sugar, butter and milk. Boil, stirring constantly, one minute. Remove from heat; stir in chocolate chips until smooth. Frost partially cooled bar.

CHERRIES A LA RHONY

6 tablespoons butter or margarine, melted
2 cups soft bread crumbs
1 (16 ounce) can tart cherries, drained
1 (16 ounce) can apricot halves, drained
1/2 cup brown sugar
1/2 tablespoon lemon juice
1 teaspoon grated lemon rind
1/2 teaspoon cinnamon
1/2 teaspoon nutmeg
1/4 teaspoon salt

Pour butter over crumbs and mix thoroughly. Put a layer of crumbs in a greased 8-inch square pan, then a layer of fruit; sprinkle with sugar, lemon juice, rind, spices and salt. Repeat until ingredients are used up. Sprinkle a few bread crumbs over top. Bake at 375 degrees for about 30 minutes. Serve plain or topped with ice cream, or whipped cream, if desired.

CHERRY CREPE FLAMBE

Crepe:
3/4 cup milk
3/4 water
3 egg yolks
1 tablespoon sugar
3 tablespoons kirsch
1 1/2 cups flour
5 tablespoons butter or margarine, melted

Spread:
3/4 cup butter or margarine
1/2 teaspoon almond flavoring
1/2 cup sugar
1/4 cup kirsch

Cherry Sauce:
1/3 cup sugar
3/4 cup water
2 cups tart cherries
1 teaspoon cornstarch
1 tablespoon cold water
1 teaspoon lemon juice
1 teaspoon almond extract
1/4 cup kirsch

Crepe:
Combine ingredients in mixing bowl or blender jar; beat until smooth. Refrigerate 2 hours or overnight. Lightly grease a 6 or 7-inch pan. Spoon about 2 tablespoons batter into pan; run around edges until solid and brown on edges. Turn when brown. Fold in half, then in half again; keep warm in oven until ready to use. Repeat for each crepe.

Spread:
Combine ingredients in bowl which is sitting in warm water. Mix well. Butter crepes before serving.

Cherry Sauce:
Boil sugar in water 5 minutes. Add cherries; cook 5 minutes. Combine cornstarch and cold water. Add to syrup; cook until clear and slightly thickened. Stir in lemon juice and almond extract.

Put buttered crepes in chaffing dish. Pour sauce over them. Heat kirsch until steaming. Pour over sauce; ignite.

CHERRY BROWN BETTY

1 cup rolled oats
1 cup flour
3/4 cup packed brown sugar
1/2 teaspoon cinnamon
1/2 cup butter or margarine
1 (21 ounce) can cherry pie filling

Combine oats, flour, sugar and cinnamon. Cut in butter with fork or pastry blender until particles are fine. Spread half the oat mixture in 9-inch square baking pan. Cover with pie filling; sprinkle with remaining oat mixture. Bake at 375 degrees for 40 minutes. Serve slightly warm topped with ice cream, or whipped topping, if desired.

CHERRY BREEZE

1 cup graham cracker crumbs
1/3 cup soft butter or margarine softened
8 ounces cream cheese, softened
1 (14 ounce) can condensed milk
1/3 cup lemon juice
1 (21 ounce) can cherry pie filling

Combine crumbs and butter, pat into bottom of 9-inch square pan. Whip cream cheese; add condensed milk, and beat until smooth. Add lemon juice and continue mixing. Spread over crumbs. Top with cherry pie filling. Chill several hours before serving.

CHERRY-MALLOW DESSERT

Graham cracker crust:
1 1/2 cups graham cracker crumbs
2 tablespoons sugar
1/3 cup butter or margarine, melted

Filling:
1/2 pint whipping cream
1 cup miniature marshmallows
1 (21 -ounce) can cherry pie filling

Crust:
Combine crumbs, sugar and butter; press firmly into a 9-inch square pan. Bake at 400 degrees for 10 minutes. Chill 1 hour.

Filling:
Whip cream until stiff peaks form. Fold in miniature marshmallows and pie filling. Spread over crust. Chill until firm. Cut into squares for serving.

CHERRY DESSERT

Filling:
1 (16 ounce) can tart cherries
3/4 cup sugar
2 tablespoons tapioca
1/2 teaspoon cinnamon
1 teaspoon almond extract 1/4 teaspoon red food coloring, optional

Crust:
1/2 cup brown sugar
1 cup flour
1/8 teaspoon salt
1/2 teaspoon baking soda
1 cup rolled oats
1/2 cup butter or margarine

Filling:
Drain cherries, reserving juice. In saucepan, combine sugar, tapioca, and cinnamon. Stir in juice. Cook and stir until mixture comes to a full rolling boil. Remove from heat. Stir in cherries, extract and food coloring. Set aside to cool.

Crust:
Combine dry ingredients. Melt butter and mix in. Pat half the mixture into an even layer in the bottom of an 8-inch square pan. Pour cherry mixture over first layer. Sprinkle remaining crumb mixture over cherries. Bake at 350 degrees for about 30 minutes.

CHERRY-CHEESE DESSERT

1 1/2 cups graham cracker crumbs
3 tablespoons sugar
6 tablespoons butter or margarine
1 (32 ounce) can cherry pie filling
2 cups whipped dessert topping
3 tablespoons powdered sugar
3 ounces cream cheese, softened

Combine graham cracker crumbs, sugar and butter. Reserve 1/4 cup mixture; pack remainder into bottom of a 9-inch square pan. Spread cherry pie filling over crumbs. Mix whipped dessert topping, powdered sugar and cream cheese. Spread over pie filling. Sprinkle reserved crumbs over top. Chill until firm.

BAKED CHERRY SHORTBREAD

1/2 cup shortening
1 1/4 cups flour
2 tablespoons sugar
1 (3 1/4 ounce) package vanilla pudding mix
1 3/4 cups milk
1 teaspoon vanilla extract
1 (21 ounce) can cherry pie filling

Cut shortening into flour and sugar until the mixture resembles coarse corn meal. Pack into 8 inch square pan. Bake at 400 degrees for 20 to 25 minutes. Cool.

Prepare pudding according to package directions with milk; add vanilla. Cool. Spread pudding over crumb mixture. Top with pie filling. Chill.

CHERRY FLUFF

1 (16 ounce) can tart cherries
1 envelope unflavored gelatin
3/4 cup sugar
1/2 teaspoon almond extract
1 cup heavy cream, whipped
20 vanilla wafers, crushed

Drain cherries, reserving juice. Soak gelatin in 1/4 cup cherry juice 5 minutes. Cut cherries fine with scissors. Heat remaining cherry juice with sugar to boiling point. Add softened gelatin and almond extract, stirring until gelatin dissolves. Chill until it starts to congeal. Add cherries. Fold in whipped cream. Sprinkle half the crumbs in the bottom of an 8 x 8 x 2-inch pan. Pour in cherry mixture. Sprinkle remaining crumbs over top mixture. Chill several hours. Cut in squares to serve.

Baking Made Simple...

To cut a cake without breaking the icing, wet the knife in boiling water first.

Pastry should be rolled out between 2 sheets of waxed paper, remove the top sheet to use the pastry for a pie plate.

CHERRY PUFFS

Puffs:
1 (16-ounce) can tart cherries
1/4 teaspoon almond extract
1 tablespoon lemon juice
1/4 teaspoon red food coloring
1/3 cup shortening
2/3 cup sugar
1/2 teaspoon almond extract
1 egg
1/2 teaspoon baking powder
1 cup flour
1/2 teaspoon salt
1/3 cup milk

Cherry Sauce:
1/4 cup sugar
1 tablespoon cornstarch
Juice from drained cherries
Water
1/4 teaspoon red food coloring

Puffs:
Drain cherries, reserving liquid. Mix together cherries, almond extract, lemon juice and food coloring. Put in bottom of 6 deep or 8 shallow greased custard cups. Using electric beater, cream shortening, beat sugar in gradually. Add almond extract and egg; beat well. Sift baking powder, flour and salt together; add alternately with milk. Pour over cherries, filling each cup half full. Bake at 375 degrees for 25 to 30 minutes.

Cherry Sauce:
Combine sugar and cornstarch in saucepan. Stir in reserved cherry juice plus water to make 1 cup and add food coloring. Cook until clear and thickened, about 10 minutes, stirring constantly. Turn out puffs and top with sauce. Serve warm.

CHERRY-BANANA PUFF

1 1/3 cups sugar
1/4 cup quick cooking tapioca
1 (16-ounce) cans tart cherries, undrained
2 cups sliced bananas (3 medium bananas)
4 egg whites
1/2 teaspoon cream of tartar
1/4 teaspoon salt
4 egg yolks
2/3 cup sugar
3/4 cup sifted cake flour

In electric skillet, combine 1 1/3 cups sugar and tapioca; stir in undrained cherries. Let stand 5 minutes. Add bananas; bring mixture to boiling. Reduce heat; cook and stir until mixture is thickened and bubbly. Keep warm. Beat egg whites until foamy; add cream of tartar and salt, beating to stiff peaks. Beat egg yolks until thick and lemon-colored; gradually add 2/3 cup sugar, beating thoroughly. Fold yolk mixture into egg whites; fold in flour. Spread over cherry mixture in skillet. Cover skillet. Simmer (220 degrees) for 25 - 30 minutes. Sprinkle top lightly with additional sugar and ground cinnamon, if desired. Serve warm.

Makes 12 serving.

CHERRY PINWHEELS

Pinwheels:
2 cups flour
3 1/2 teaspoons baking powder
3/4 teaspoon salt
3 tablespoons sugar
6 tablespoons shortening
1 egg slightly beaten
Milk
1 1/2 cups drained tart cherries, (reserve liquid)
1/4 cup sugar

Sauce:
3/4 cup sugar
1 1/2 tablespoons cornstarch
1 cup cherry liquid
2 tablespoons lemon juice
Red food coloring, if desired

Pinwheels:
Sift together flour, baking powder, salt, and sugar. Cut in shortening until it resembles coarse corn meal. Add enough milk to the beaten egg to make 3/4 cup. Add the liquid to the dry ingredients; stir with a fork until all of the dry ingredients are moistened. Turn dough onto floured board. Knead lightly for about 1/2 minute. Pat or roll into an oblong shape about 10 x 20 inches and 1/4 inch thick. Cover with cherries; sprinkle sugar over cherries. Roll as for jelly roll. Pinch long edge to side of roll. Cut in about 1-inch slices. Put close together in greased 9-inch round baking dish or in well-greased muffin pans. Bake at 400 degrees 20 to 25 minutes. Serve warm with sauce.

CHERRY DUMP PUDDING

1 cup flour
1/4 teaspoon salt
1 teaspoon baking powder
1/2 cup sugar
1 cup milk

1/4 teaspoon vanilla
2 cups tart cherries
1/4 cup sugar
1 cup hot water or cherry juice

Sift together flour, salt, baking powder and 1/2 cup sugar. Add shortening, milk and vanilla; beat 2 minutes. Pour into greased 6 x 10-inch pan; cover with cherries. Sprinkle with 1/4 cup sugar. Cover this with hot liquid. Bake at 375 degrees for about 40 minutes. Serve warm, plain or with whipped cream.

CHERRY DUMPLINGS

1 (16 ounce) can tart cherries, (1 1/2 cups)
2 tablespoons butter or margarine
1/3 cup sugar
1 (10 count) can refrigerator biscuits
5 teaspoons butter or margarine
7 tablespoons sugar

Drain cherries, reserving juice; combine juice with 2 tablespoons butter and 1/3 cup sugar; heat to boiling. Roll out each biscuit to about 4 inches in diameter. In center of each biscuit, put 2 tablespoons of cherries; top each mound with 1/2 teaspoon butter and 2 teaspoons sugar. Bring edges of dough to a point on top of cherries, carefully seal edges. Put in a greased 8-inch square pan. Pour hot cherry juice around dumplings. Bake at 375 degrees for 25 to 30 minutes. Serve warm with cream, if desired.

CHERRY CHOCOLATE CREAM

1 teaspoon cocoa
1 cup whipping cream, whipped
2 cups chocolate wafers, coarsely broken
1/3 cup cherry preserves

Add cocoa to whipped cream. Combine half of whipped cream with wafers. Put 2 tablespoons of wafer mixture into 4 sherbert glasses; top with 1 tablespoon preserves. Add remaining wafer mixture; top with remaining whipped cream. Garnish with 1 teaspoon preserves. Keep chilled.

SWEET CHERRY CREAM

3/4 cup sugar
1 envelope unflavored gelatin
1 1/2 cups water
1 cup sour cream
1 1/2 teaspoons vanilla
1 cup whipped dessert topping
2 cans dark sweet cherries, drained and blotted

In saucepan, combine sugar and gelatin; stir in water. Over low heat, stir to dissolve sugar and gelatin. Remove from heat. Blend in sour cream and vanilla. Chill until slightly thickened. Fold in dessert topping and cherries. Pour into 2 quart oiled mold and chill until firm, about 4 hours.

CHERRIES A LA CREME

1 (3 ounce) package cherry gelatin
1 cup boiling water
1/2 cup orange juice
2 tablespoons lemon juice
1 (16 ounce) can dark sweet cherries, drained and sliced
1/4 cup chopped toasted almonds
1 cup whipping cream, whipped
1/4 teaspoon almond extract

Dissolve gelatin in boiling water. Add fruit juices. Chill until partially set. Beat gelatin until light and fluffy. Fold in cherries, almonds, whipped cream and extract. Pour into greased individual or 1 1/2 quart mold. Chill until firm. Unmold onto plate and garnish with fresh cherries with stems.

CHERRY CREAM PARFAITS

1 cup milk
1 cup sour cream
1/4 teaspoon almond extract
1 (3 1/4 ounce) package instant vanilla pudding
1 (21 ounce) can cherry pie filling

Combine milk, sour cream and almond extract. Add pudding and beat 2 minutes. Fill parfait (4 large or 6 small) glasses with alternate layers of cherries and pudding. Chill.

CELESTIAL RICE DESSERT

Rice Dessert:
3 1/2 cups cooked rice, cooled
1 1/2 cups sifted powdered sugar
1 tablespoon rum flavoring
2 tablespoons vanilla
2 tablespoons cherry gelatin
1/2 cup cold water
1/2 cup half & half

2 cups whipping cream, whipped
Whole maraschino cherries

Cherry Sauce:
2 tablespoons cornstarch
1 1/2 cups water
1 cup maraschino cherry syrup
2 tablespoons lemon juice

Rice Dessert:
Combine rice, powdered sugar, rum flavoring, and vanilla. Soften gelatin in cold water; blend in cream. Cook over low heat until gelatin is dissolved, stirring constantly. Cool. Blend into rice mixture. Chill until slightly thickened, stirring occasionally. Fold whipped cream and cherries into thickened rice. Spoon into individual dessert dishes or layer with cherry sauce in parfait glasses.

Cherry Sauce:
Mix cornstarch and water in saucepan. Add cherry syrup; bring mixture to boil, boil for 3 minutes, stirring constantly. Cool. Add lemon juice. Serve with rice dessert.

CHERRY BAVARIAN

1 envelope unflavored gelatin
1/3 cup sugar
1/8 teaspoon salt
1 (16-ounce) can red tart cherries
2 eggs, separated
1/4 teaspoon almond flavoring
1/4 teaspoon red food coloring
1/3 cup sugar
1 cup heavy cream, whipped

Mix gelatin, 1/3 cup sugar and salt in saucepan. Drain cherries; beat together cherry liquid and egg yolks; add to gelatin mixture. On low heat, stir constantly until gelatin and sugar are dissolved, about 5 minutes. Remove from heat; add almond flavoring, food coloring and cherries. Chill until mixture mounds slightly when dropped from a spoon.

Beat egg whites until stiff, but not dry. Gradually add 1/3 cup sugar and beat until very stiff. Fold into cherry mixture; fold in whipped cream. Pour into a 6-cup mold; chill until firm.

CHERRY TAPIOCA

1 (16-ounce) can tart cherries
3/4 cup sugar
1/4 cup quick cooking tapioca
1/8 teaspoon salt

1/4 teaspoon red food coloring
1/8 teaspoon almond extract
1/3 heavy cream, whipped

Drain cherries; add waters to cherry juice to make 2 cups liquid. Add sugar, tapioca and salt to liquid; cook, stirring occasionally. Add cherries, food coloring and almond extract. Chill. Just before serving, fold in the whipped cream.
Note: when using sweetened frozen cherries, reduce sugar to 1/2 cup.

EGGNOG PUDDING WITH CHERRY SAUCE

Pudding:
2 tablespoons sugar
1 envelope (1 tablespoon) unflavored gelatin
Dash salt
2 egg yolks
1 1/2 cups milk
2 egg whites
1/4 cup sugar
1/4 teaspoon nutmeg
1/4 teaspoon rum flavoring

Sauce:
1 (16 ounce) can tart cherries
1/2 cup sugar
1/2 cup orange marmalade
2 tablespoons cornstarch
Few drops red food coloring
1/3 cup toasted silvered almonds

Pudding:
Combine 2 tablespoons sugar, gelatin, and salt. Beat egg yolks and milk together; add gelatin. Cook over simmering water or low heat until gelatin dissolves and mixture coats a metal spoon. Chill until mixture begins to thicken. Beat egg whites until fluffy; add 1/4 cup sugar gradually and beat until stiff. Fold egg whites into gelatin mixture; add nutmeg and flavoring. Pour into a one quart mold or individual molds or use single serving dishes. Chill overnight or until firm.

Sauce:
Drain cherries, reserving 1/2 cup juice. Combine cherries, sugar and marmalade; heat until sugar dissolves. Blend cornstarch with a small amount of juice; combine with remaining juice and cook, stirring constantly until mixture is thick and clear. Add cherry mixture, red food coloring, and almonds. Serve over unmolded pudding.

CHERRIES JUBILEE

1 (16-ounce) can dark sweet cherries
1/2 cup sugar
Dash salt
1 tablespoon cornstarch
1 cup water
3 tablespoons brandy
1 pint vanilla ice cream

Drain cherries, reserving juice. Combine sugar, salt, cornstarch and water. Add cherry juice; cook until thickened, stirring constantly. Add cherries. Pour brandy over top, ignite brandy, and spoon immediately over ice cream.

BING CHERRY ICE CREAM

2 eggs
1/2 cup sugar
2 1/2 cups half & half

1/4 teaspoon red food coloring
2 cups dark sweet cherries, halved
2 teaspoons vanilla

Beat eggs until lemon colored. Gradually add sugar; continue beating until thick. Stir in half & half, vanilla, coloring and cherries. For freezing, follow directions with ice cream freezer. Store in sealed containers.

CHERRY CREAM SHERBERT

1 (16-ounce) can tart cherries
2/3 cup sugar
1/2 teaspoon salt
1 teaspoon lemon juice
1/4 teaspoon almond extract
1/4 teaspoon red food coloring
1 tablespoon granulated gelatin
1/4 cup cold water
1 cup whipping cream
Green maraschino cherries, optional

Thoroughly drain juice from cherries. Put drained cherries through food processor using fine blade, catching any juice dripping from food processor; or blend contents of can of medium speed in blender jar. Combine ground cherries, sugar, salt, lemon juice, almond extract and red food coloring. Soften gelatin in cold water 5 minutes, then place over hot water to melt. Pour gelatin slowly into cherry mixture, stirring constantly. Refrigerate until mixture starts to congeal. Whip cream until stiff, fold in cherry mixture. Pour into 8-inch square pan and refrigerate. Serve on chilled serving dishes with a sliced green maraschino cherry. Keeps well in freezer.

MINTED CHOCOLATE CHIP CHERRY ICE CREAM

1 1/2 teaspoons cornstarch
1/4 teaspoon salt
3/4 cup sugar
2 cups milk
2 eggs, separated
3 - 4 drops mint flavoring
3 - 4 drops green food coloring
2/3 cup chopped green maraschino cherries (about 25 cherries)
6 ounces semi-sweet miniature chocolate pieces
1 cup heavy cream, whipped

Blend cornstarch, salt and sugar; add milk and stir. Cook over low heat until slightly thickened, stirring constantly. Beat egg yolks; gradually add a little of hot mixture to egg yolks, mix well and add to remaining hot mixture; cook over low heat 3 - 4 minutes, stirring constantly. Cool.

Add flavoring and coloring; beat until smooth. Beat egg whites until stiff but not dry; fold egg whites and remaining ingredients into thoroughly cooled mixture. For freezing follow directions with ice cream freezer. Store in sealed containers.

CHERRY SKILLET DESSERT

1/2 cup butter or margarine
1 1/2 cups graham cracker crumbs
1/2 cup sugar

8 ounces cream cheese, softened
1/2 cup sugar
2 eggs
1 (21-ounce) can cherry pie filling

Melt butter in 10-inch skillet. Remove from heat. Mix in crumbs and 1/2 cup sugar. Pat mixture on bottom of skillet firmly.

Cream cheese until smooth; gradually beat in 1/2 cup sugar. Add eggs one at a time; mix well after each addition. Beat mixture until very smooth. Pour over crumbs. Bake at 250 degrees for 25 minutes. Remove from oven and cool. Spoon cherry filling over top. Chill at least 3 hours before serving. Dollop with whipped cream, if desired.

Cookie Tip...

When using plastic cookie cutters, they should be dipped in warm vegetable oil while you are working. You will get a cleaner, more defined edge on the patterns.

KASKÜCHEN

Pastry:
1/3 cup butter or margarine
1/3 cup sugar
1 egg
1 1/4 cups flour

Filling:
24 ounces cream cheese, softened
3/4 cup sugar
2 tablespoons flour
1 teaspoon vanilla
3 eggs
2 tablespoons milk
1 (21-ounce) can cherry pie filling

Pastry:
Cream butter and sugar until light and fluffy; blend in egg. Add flour; mix well. Spread dough with spatula on bottom and 1 1/2 inches high around sides of a 9-inch spring-form pan. Prick as for crust.

Filling:
Combine cream cheese, sugar, flour and vanilla until well blended. Add eggs one at a time, mixing well after each addition. Blend in milk, pour into pastry-lined pan; bake at 450 degrees for 10 minutes. Reduce heat to 250 degrees; continue baking for 35 - 40 minutes. Loosen cake from rim of pan; cool before removing rim of pan. Chill. Spread with pie filling to serve.

PETITE CHERRY CHEESE CAKES

1 cup vanilla wafer crumbs
3 1/2 tablespoons butter or margarine, melted
8 ounces cream cheese, softened
1/3 cup sugar
1 egg
2 teaspoons lemon juice
1/2 teaspoon vanilla extract
1 (21-ounce) can cherry pie filling

Line 12 muffin cups with aluminum cupcake papers. Combine crumbs and butter. Spoon about 1 tablespoon crumb mixture into bottom of each cup and press gently. Beat cream cheese until fluffy. Add sugar, egg, lemon juice and vanilla; beat until smooth. Spoon evenly into crumb-lined paper lined paper cups. Bake at 375 for 15 minutes or until set. Cool. Spoon pie filling over each petite cheese cake.

CHERRY COBBLER

1 (21-ounce) can cherry pie filling
1 tablespoon grated lemon peel
1 cup biscuit mix
1/4 cup butter or margarine, softened
3 tablespoons boiling water
1/2 teaspoon sugar
1/4 teaspoon cinnamon

Mix pie filling and lemon peel in 8 x 8 x 2-inch pan. Combine biscuit mix and butter. Add water; stir vigorously until dough forms a ball and cleans the bowl. Drop dough by spoonsful onto fruit mixture. Mix sugar and cinnamon; sprinkle over dough. Bake at 400 degrees for 25 - 30 minutes or until topping is golden brown. Serve warm.

CHERRY & CREAM CHEESE CAKE

Crust:
1 cup graham cracker crumbs
2 tablespoons sugar
1/3 cup butter or margarine, melted

Filling:
2 envelopes unflavored gelatin
3/4 cup sugar
1/4 teaspoon salt
3 egg yolks
1 cup milk
3 (8-ounce) packages softened cream cheese
2 tablespoons grated lemon peel
2 tablespoons lemon juice
1 teaspoon vanilla
3 egg whites (room temperature)
1/4 cup sugar
1 cup sour cream

Glaze:
1 (21-ounce) can cherry pie filling

Crust:
Combine ingredients; mix well with fork. Reserve 1/4 cup. Pat remainder in bottom of a 9 x 3-inch spring-form pan. Refrigerate.

Filling:
In a small saucepan, combine gelatin, sugar and salt. In a small bowl, with wire whisk, beat egg yolks with milk until smooth; gradually add to gelatin mixture; mix

well. Over medium heat, stir until gelatin is dissolved and custard is thickened slightly (should form coating on metal spoon), about 5 minutes. Remove from heat; cool 10 minutes.

In large bowl, beat cream cheese, lemon peel, lemon juice and vanilla until smooth, about 3 minutes. Slowly add cooled custard, beating at low speed to blend. Set in a bowl of ice water to chill, stirring occasionally, until mixture mounds when lifted with spoon (partially set).

Beat egg whites until soft peaks form. Gradually add 1/4 cup sugar, beating until stiff peaks form. Fold beaten egg whites and sour cream into cheese mixture just until smooth. Pour over crust. Refrigerate at least 4 hours or overnight.

Glaze:
Spread glaze over top of cheese cake just before serving.

FESTIVE UPSIDE DOWN CAKE

1 cup light brown sugar
3/4 cup chopped nuts
1/2 cup plus 1 tablespoon butter or margarine, melted
1 (2 layer size) white or yellow cake mix
1 1/2 cups (13 ounces) sliced maraschino cherries
Eggs as directed
3 tablespoons maraschino cherry syrup
2 cups whipped dessert topping

Combine brown sugar and melted butter in a bowl.
Stir in cherries, cherry syrup and nuts. Spread this mixture evenly in bottom of two 8 or 9-inch layer pans. Prepare cake as directed on package, using 3 tablespoons cherry syrup in place of equal amount of liquid called for. Carefully pour cake batter over brown sugar mixture and bake according to package directions. Let stand in pans on wire rack for 10 minutes; invert onto rack. Let stand a minute; then remove pans. Cool thoroughly. Put one cake layer with cherry side up on a serving plate; top with second layer with cherry side up. Frost sides and garnish top with whipped topping. If preferred, whipped topping may be placed between layers rather than on sides of cake.

MAGIC CHERRY UPSIDE DOWN CAKE

1 (2 layer) white or yellow cake mix
Eggs as directed
1 (16-ounce) can tart cherries
1 1/2 cups sugar
1 teaspoon almond extract
1 teaspoon red food coloring
2 tablespoons cornstarch
1 tablespoon butter or margarine, melted

Prepare cake with eggs as directed on package. Pour into greased 9 x 13 x 2-inch pan. mix undrained cherries, sugar, extract, food coloring, cornstarch and butter. Pour evenly over batter. Bake at 350 degrees about 50 minutes. Serve warm or cold with ice cream or whipped cream, if desired.

CHERRY ALMOND FUDGE CAKE

Cake:
1 (2 layer) chocolate fudge cake mix
Eggs as directed
1 teaspoon almond extract
1 (21-ounce) can cherry pie filling

Frosting:
1 cup granulated sugar
1/2 cup butter or margarine
1/2 cup shortening
1/2 cup milk
1/2 teaspoon almond extract

Cake:
Prepare cake as directed on box. Stir in almond extract and 1 cup cherry pie filling. Bake in 9-inch round layer pans as directed. When cool, spread remaining cherry filling between layers.

Frosting:
Combine all ingredients. Beat on high speed for 15 minutes. Cake must be completely cooled before frosting sides and top. Garnish with halved maraschino cherry "flowers", if desired.

BLACK CHERRY CREAM TRIFLE

12 ounces pound cake, sliced into 1/4 to 3/8 inch slices
2 (16-ounce) cans dark sweet cherries
1 (6-ounce) package black cherry gelatin
1 cup boiling water
4 cups whipped dessert topping

Line bottom and sides of 9-inch spring form pan or glass serving bowl with slices of pound cake. Thoroughly drain cherries, reserving juice; add enough to make 2 cups liquid. Dissolve gelatin in 1 cup boiling water; add the 2 cups cherry juice. Let cool until thick and syrupy.

Fold in whipped topping and drained cherries, reserving enough cream and cherries for garnish, if desired. Pour into prepared pan and chill several hours or overnight. Remove from pan to serving plate; garnish with topping and cherries.

Makes 16 servings.

CHERRY BAKED ALASKA

9-inch cake layer, any flavor
1 quart vanilla ice cream, softened
1 (12-ounce) jar cherry preserves
1/4 cup slivered almonds, toasted
2/3 cup egg whites (5 - 7 eggs)
2/3 cup sugar

Put cake on heat proof plate or cookie sheet.

Line deep 1 1/2 quart bowl with aluminum foil or plastic wrap; chill. Swirl through the ice cream 1/2 of the cherry preserves and the almonds. Pack smoothly into chilled bowl and freeze until very firm.

Beat egg whites until soft peaks form; gradually add sugar, beating stiff peaks. Invert bowl of ice cream onto cake layer, lift off bowl and peel off foil. Quickly cover ice cream and cake base with meringue, making sure there are no gaps in meringue covering.

With Alaska low in oven, bake at 500 degrees (oven preheated) for 3 minutes or until meringue is golden brown. Heat remaining cherry preserves and drizzle over Alaska just before serving.

Makes 12 servings. Can be returned to freezer either before or after baking meringue.

CHERRY SAVARIN CHANTILLY

Cake:
1 envelope dry yeast
2 tablespoons sugar
1/4 cup very warm water
1/4 teaspoon salt
3 eggs
2 1/2 cups flour
1 teaspoon grated lemon rind
6 tablespoons butter or margarine, softened

Cherry Glaze:
1 (12-ounce) jar cherry preserves
1/4 teaspoon almond extract

Creme Chantilly:
2 tablespoons powdered sugar
2 teaspoons vanilla
1 cup whipping cream, whipped

Cherry Savarin Syrup:
1/2 cup sugar
1 cup water
1/8 teaspoon almond extract

Cake:
Dissolve yeast and 1/2 teaspoon sugar in water; let stand 10 minutes. Combine yeast, remaining sugar, salt, eggs, 2 cups flour and lemon rind. Add butter one tablespoon at a time, beating well after each addition. Stir in remaining flour. Turn into a greased bundt pan or 8 1/2-inch tube pan. Let rise in warm place 45 minutes or until double in bulk. Bake at 375 degrees for 35 minutes. Remove from pan to a deep plate.

Cherry Savarin Syrup:
Combine sugar and water; bring to a boil. Cool. Add almond extract. Prick top of warm cake with skewer; drizzle with syrup.

Cherry Glaze:
Heat cherry preserves and almond flavoring. Spread on cake while still warm.

Creme Chantilly:
Fold powdered sugar and vanilla into whipped cream. When ready to serve, spoon into center of cake.

CHERRY POUND CAKE SURPRISE

1 (21-ounce) can cherry pie filling
3/4 teaspoon almond extract
1 1/2 teaspoons grated orange rink
1 (16-ounce) pound cake
2 cups whipped dessert topping
1 cup toasted flake coconut
4 or 5 mint leaves

Combine pie filling, almond extract and orange rind.

Split pound cake into 3 layers and spread between layers with pie filling (reserving 6 or 7 cherries from filling for garnishing top of dessert)

Put top layer on cake and frost entire cake generously with dessert topping.

Sprinkle sides and edges of top with toasted coconut. Garnish center of top with reserved cherries and mint leaves. Refrigerate several hours before serving.

CHERRY GLAZED POUND CAKE

Cake:
2 1/3 cups flour
1 teaspoon baking powder
1/2 teaspoon salt
1 1/4 cup sugar
2/3 cup butter or margarine, softened
3 eggs
1/2 cup milk
1 teaspoon grated lemon rind
1 tablespoon lemon juice

Cherry Honey Glaze:
1 (21-ounce) can cherry pie filling
1 tablespoon lemon juice
2 tablespoons honey

Cake: Sift together flour, baking powder and salt. Cream butter, sugar, and eggs. Combine milk, lemon rind and lemon juice. To creamed mixture, add flour and milk mixtures alternately by hand. Pour into greased and floured 10-inch bundt or 9-inch tube pan; bake at 350 degrees for about 1 hour.

Cherry Honey Glaze;
Combine ingredients; simmer over low heat for 5 minutes. To serve, drizzle over pound cake.

Baking To Perfection...

When a cherry cake is browning too quickly, place a small pan of warm water above it in the oven.

Cherry cookies that have become soft can be crisped up by placing them into a low temperature oven for 5 minutes.

CHERRY COFFEE CAKE

Filling:*
1/4 cup cornstarch
1/2 cup sugar
1/4 teaspoon salt
1 (16-ounce) can tart cherries
Red food coloring
1 tablespoon grated orange peel

Coffee Cake:
1 package dry yeast
1/4 cup warm water
1/2 cup butter or margarine
1/2 cup sugar
3 eggs, slightly beaten
1/4 cup milk
3 cups sifted flour
1/2 teaspoon salt
2 tablespoons flour

Filling:
Combine cornstarch, sugar and salt in saucepan. Drain cherries, reserving juice. Add enough water to juice to make 1 cup liquid. Slowly stir liquid into cornstarch mixture. Add red food coloring. Mix well, stirring constantly, until mixture comes to a boil and thickens. Remove from heat. Stir in cherries and orange peel. Set aside to cool.

*Note: For a quick filling, use 1 (21-ounces) cherry pie filling. Boil 3 minutes, stirring constantly. Cool.

Coffee Cake:
Sprinkle yeast over warm water; stir until dissolved. Cream butter, adding sugar gradually. Stir in yeast mixture, eggs, milk, 3 cups flour and salt. Beat until well-blended. Set aside 1/2 cup dough. Spread remaining dough in greased 9 x 9 x 2 - inch pan. Spread topping over dough. Work 1/2 cup dough. Work 1/2 cup dough with 2 tablespoons flour. Roll into a rectangle. Cut with cookie cutters, making stars (or other suitable design). Arrange the design over cherry filling. Cover, let rise in warm place until doubled in bulk, about 1 hour. Bake at 375 degrees 35 - 40 minutes.

CHERRY PUDDING CAKE

1 1/4 cups sugar
1 cup flour
1 teaspoon baking soda
1 teaspoon cinnamon
1/2 teaspoon salt
1 egg, beaten
2 cups drained tart cherries
1/2 cup chopped nuts

Sift together dry ingredients. Mix in egg, cherries and nuts. Pour into greased and floured 9-inch square pan. Bake at 350 degrees for 45 minutes. Let stand in pan for 10 minutes before turning out onto serving platter. Garnish with whipped topping, if desired.

CHERRY COTTAGE PUDDING

Cake:
1 1/2 cups tart cherries, chop, drain, reserving liquid
1/2 cup granulated sugar

6 tablespoons butter or margarine
1/3 cup granulated sugar
1 egg
1 3/4 cups flour
2 1/2 teaspoons baking powder
1/2 teaspoon salt

Sauce:
2 tablespoons cornstarch
2 tablespoons granulated sugar
1/8 teaspoon salt
1 1/4 cups reserved cherry liquid and water
1 cup tart cherries, drained
1/4 teaspoon almond extract
4 drops red food coloring

Cake:
Combine cherries and 1/2 cup granulated sugar; let stand about 10 minutes. Drain, reserving liquid.

Cream together butter, 1/3 cup granulated sugar and brown sugar. Add egg; beat well. Sift together flour, baking powder and salt. Add to creamed mixture alternately with milk, beating well. Fold in drained cherries. Pour into greased and floured 9 x 9 x 2-inch pan. Bake at 350 degrees for 35 to 40 minutes, or until cake tests done. Serve with sauce.

Sauce:
In saucepan, combine cornstarch, sugar and salt. Slowly add cherry liquid stirring to make smooth paste. Cook and stir until thickened and bubbly. Add cherries, almond extract and food coloring. Cool slightly. Serve over pudding.

Makes bout 1 1/2 cups sauce.

CHERRY COFFEE CAKE ROYALE

Cake:
1/2 cup butter or margarine
1 cup granulated sugar
2 eggs
1 teaspoon vanilla
2 cups flour
1/2 teaspoon baking soda
1/2 teaspoon baking powder
1/2 teaspoon salt
1 cup sour cream
1 (21-ounce) can cherry pie filling

Topping:
1/4 cup granulated sugar
1/4 cup brown sugar
1/2 cup flour
1 teaspoon cinnamon
1/4 cup chopped nuts
1/3 cup butter or margarine

Cake:
Cream together butter, sugar, eggs and vanilla. Sift together flour, baking soda, baking powder and salt. Combine the sifted dry ingredients and the sour cream alternately with the creamed mixture. Spread half of this batter in the bottom of a

greased and floured 9 x 13-inch pan. Carefully spread the cherry pie filling over the batter layer. Spread the remaining batter over the cherry filling.

Topping:
With pastry fork or blender, combine all ingredients to make a crumb topping. Sprinkle the topping evenly over the cake. Bake at 350 degrees for 45 to 60 minutes of until the center tests done with a toothpick.

CHERRY LOG DREAM CAKE

Cake:
1 (2 layer size) lemon cake mix
1 (2-ounce) envelope whipped topping mix
4 eggs
1 cup cold tap water
Confectioner's sugar
2 quarts softened cherry-vanilla ice cream

Brandy Cherry Sauce:
1 tablespoon sugar
1 tablespoon cornstarch
1 cup water
2 1/2 cups frozen sweet cherries
1/4 cup brandy

Cake:
Combine cake mix, dry whipped topping mix, eggs and water. Blend until moistened. Beat at medium speed for 4 minutes. Pour into two greased and floured 15 x 10-inch jelly roll pans. Bake at 350 degrees for 12 - 14 minutes. Iimmediately turn out onto cloths which have been sprinkled with confectioner's sugar. Quickly trim off crisp edges of each cake. Starting with long side, roll cake and cloth together. Cool on racks. Unroll and remove towel. Spread with ice cream. Roll cake up and store in freezer until ready to serve.

Brandy Cherry Sauce:
Combine sugar and cornstarch in saucepan. Gradually stir in water. Add cherries; cook and stir over medium heat until slightly thickened. In another saucepan, heat brandy; pour over sauce (do not stir in); ignite. Spoon over cake slices for serving.

CHERRY LAYERED ANGEL FOOD

1 angel food cake, loaf or tube
1 (3 1/4 ounce) package instant vanilla pudding
2 cups milk
1/4 cup slivered toasted almonds
1 (21-ounce) can cherry pie filling
1 cup heavy cream
Confectioner's sugar

Slice cake crosswise into 3 layers. Prepare pudding with milk as directed on package. Add toasted almonds. Spread half of mixture on bottom cake layer; top with half of cherry pie filling. Repeat on second layer. Whip heavy cream and sweeten to taste with confectioner's sugar; frost top and sides of cake. Garnish with cherries and almonds, if desired. Refrigerate.

CHERRY ROLL CAKE

Cake:
5 egg yolks
1/4 cup plus 1 tablespoon cold water
1 cup sugar
1 cup sifted cake flour
2 teaspoons baking powder
1/4 teaspoon salt
5 egg whites
1 teaspoon vanilla

Cherry Filling:
1 (21-ounce) can cherry pie filling
4 drops almond extract

Cake:
Combine egg yolks and water; beat until peaks form. Gradually add sugar. Sift together flour, baking powder and salt. Add flour mixture to egg yolk mixture. Beat egg whites and vanilla until stiff peaks form. Fold into egg yolk mixture. Spread batter in wax-paper lined 10 1/2 x 15-inch jelly roll pan. Bake at 350 degrees for 20 minutes.

Loosen sides and turn out immediately onto a towel sprinkled with confectioner's sugar. Remove wax paper and trim crusts. Roll quickly with fresh sheet of wax paper on inside of roll. Wrap in a towel sprinkled with confectioner's sugar. Cool on a cake rack. Unroll; remove paper.

Cherry Filling;
Combine ingredients and heat to boiling, stirring constantly. Cool. Spread on unrolled cake. Roll cake again. Sprinkle with confectioner's sugar.

CHERRY DEVILICIOUS CAKE

Cake:
1 (2 layer) devils food cake mix
1 (3-ounce) box instant chocolate pudding
4 eggs
1 cup hot top water
1/2 cup cooking oil
1/2 cup chopped nuts, optional

Sauce:
2 tablespoons cornstarch
2 tablespoons sugar
1 (16-ounce) can dark sweet cherries
1/4 cup burgundy

Cake:
Blend together all ingredients; beat 4 minutes. Pout into a well-greased bundt pan or 10-inch tube pan. Bake at 350 degrees for 50 - 60 minutes. Cool 10 minutes before removing from pan. (Or bake in a 9 x 13-inch pan for 35 - 40 minutes. Sift powdered sugar over top for serving.)

Sauce:
Combine cornstarch and sugar in saucepan. Add the juice from the cherries plus enough water to make 1 cup liquid. Heat and stir until thick and bubbly. Add cherries and heat through. Stir in burgundy. Serve warm sauce over cake.

PLANTATION CHERRY CAKE

1 (16-ounces) can tart cherries
1/2 cup sugar
2 2/3 cups sifted flour
1 1/2 cups sugar
4 teaspoons baking powder
1 teaspoon salt

2/3 cup shortening
1 1/3 cups milk
2 teaspoon vanilla
2 eggs
4 teaspoons cornstarch
1/4 cup toasted almonds

Combine undrained cherries and 1/2 cup sugar; heat to boiling. Cool and drain, reserving juice.

Sift together flour, 1 1/2 cups sugar, baking powder, and salt. Add shortening, milk and vanilla; beat 2 minutes. Add eggs and beat 2 minutes. Pour into greased bundt pan. Sprinkle drained cherries over batter. Bake at 350 degrees for 40 to 45 minutes, or until done. Cool 5 minutes and invert on a serving plate.

Combine a small amount of cherry juice with cornstarch in a saucepan; add remaining juice. Cook, stirring constantly, until thickened. Spoon over cake; sprinkle with toasted almonds. Serve warm.

CHERRY CROWN CAKE

1 (2 layer) white cake mix
Eggs as directed
1/4 teaspoon almond extract
1/2 cup chopped walnuts
1/8 teaspoon red food coloring
1 (21-ounce) can cherry pie filling
1 teaspoon grated orange peel
3 - 4 cups whipped dessert topping

Prepare cake mix with eggs according to package directions, adding almond extract and walnuts to batter. Remove 1/3 batter to another bowl; stir in red food coloring. Spoon pink and white batters alternately into two greased and floured layer cake pans. Cut through batter with knife of spatula to marble. Bake according to package directions. Remove from pans; cool on racks.

Combine pie filling and orange peel. Prepare desert topping mix according to directions. Put one cake layer on serving plate. Make a border of whipped topping 1 inch wide and 1/2 inch high around upper edge of cake layer. Fill with half the cherry mixture. Top with 2nd layer cake. Make another border of whipped topping 1 inch wide and 1/2 inch high. Fill with the rest of the cherries. Frost sides with rest of whipped topping. Chill 2 to 3 hours.

CHERRY WALNUT PAN CAKE

Cake:
1 (21-ounce) can cherry pie filling
2 cups flour
1 cup sugar
1 1/2 teaspoons baking soda
1 teaspoon salt
2 eggs, beaten
1 teaspoon vanilla
2/3 cup cooking oil
1/2 cup chopped walnuts

Sour Cream Topping:
1/2 cup sugar
1/2 cup sour cream
1/2 teaspoon baking soda
1/4 cup chopped walnuts

Cake:
Spread pie filling in ungreased 13 x 9 inch pan. Combine dry ingredients; sprinkle over filling. In mixing bowl, combine eggs, vanilla, oil and walnuts; mix well. Pour over ingredients in pan. Stir until blended. Smooth batter evenly in pan. Bake at 350 degrees 40 to 50 minutes. As soon as cake is removed from oven, prick warm cake with fork.

Sour Cream Topping:
Combine sugar, sour cream and soda in saucepan. Cook over medium heat, stirring until it boils. Pour hot topping over warm cake. Sprinkle with walnuts. Serve cake warm, plain or with ice cream.

SWEET CHERRY CAKE

Cake:
1 (2 layer) white cake mix
Eggs as directed
2 cups dark sweet cherries, canned or fresh

Frosting:
1 cup chopped nuts
1 cup sugar
1 cup half & half
1 egg, well-beaten

Cake:
Prepare cake with eggs as directed on package. Pour batter into 2 greased and floured 9-inch layer pans. Arrange well drained cherries on top of each layer. Bake as directed.

Frosting:
Combine all ingredients in top of double boiler. Cook until thickened, about 10 minutes. Cool. Spread on top and between layers of cake.

CHERRY GINGERBREAD RING

1 (14 1/2-ounce) package gingerbread mix
1 egg
1/2 teaspoon salt
3/4 cup water
1 (21-ounce) can cherry pie filling
1/2 cup chopped pecans
1 cup whipped dessert topping, optional

Prepare gingerbread batter with egg according to package directions, except add the salt and use 3/4 cup water instead of liquid called for on package. Stir in 1 1/4 cups pie filling and nuts. Bake in well-greased and floured 6 1/2 cup ring mold at 375 degree for 40 - 45 minutes, (or use a 9 x 9-inch pan for 30 - 35 minutes) Loosen edges and unmold hot cake onto serving plate. Drizzle remaining cherry pie filling on cake. Serve warm with whipped topping.

CHERRY SPICE RING

1 (2 layer) spice cake mix
Eggs as directed
1 (16-ounce) can tart cherries, drained

Prepare cake with eggs as directed on package. Fold in cherries. Bake as directed. Frost with butter cream frosting flavored with almond extract, if desired.

CHERRY CRUMBLE CAKE

1 (21-ounce) can cherry pie filling
1 (20-ounce) can crushed pineapple
1 (2 layer) yellow cake mix
1 cup butter or margarine, melted
1 cup coconut

Spread cherry pie filling in bottom of 9 x 13-inch pan; pour pineapple over it. Sprinkle dry cake mix over fruit. Drizzle butter over mix. Top with coconut, bake at 350 degrees for about 35 minutes.

MARASCHINO CHERRY CAKE

Cake:
2 cups plus 2 tablespoons flour
1 1/3 cups sugar
1 teaspoon baking powder
1 teaspoon salt
1/2 cup soft shortening
3/4 cup milk
1/4 cup maraschino cherry juice
4 egg whites (1/2 cup)
16 maraschino cherries, chopped
1/2 cup chopped nuts

Frosting:
2 eggs whites
1 1/2 cups sugar
1/3 cup maraschino cherry juice
1 teaspoon vanilla
1/4 teaspoon cream of tartar

Cake:
Heat oven to 350 degrees. Grease and flour baking pan, 13 x 9 x 2, or 2 round layer pans, 8 or 9-inch. Sift flour, sugar, baking powder, and salt into large mixing bowl. Add shortening, cherry juice and 1/2 cup milk. Blend 1/2 minute on low speed to moisten. Beat 2 minutes on high speed. Add remaining milk and the egg whites; beat 2 minutes on high speed. Fold in cherries and nuts. Pour into greased and floured pans. Bake at 350 degrees for 30 to 35 minutes. Cool.

Frosting:
Combine egg whites, sugar, cream of tartar and cherry juice in top of double boiler. Beat on high speed 1 minute with electric mixer. Cook over boiling water, beating on high speed 7 minutes. Remove pan from boiling water; add vanilla. Beat 2 minutes longer on high speed. Frost cake when cool.

CHERRY CARNIVAL CAKE

Cake:
1/3 cup shortening
1 1/2 cups sugar
2 eggs
2 1/2 cups flour
1 1/2 teaspoons baking powder
1 1/2 teaspoons baking soda
1/2 teaspoon salt
1 cup milk
2 - 2 1/4 cups unsweetened tart cherries
1/2 cup chopped nuts

Hot Cherry Sauce:
1/2 cup sugar
2 tablespoons cornstarch
Few grains of salt
3/4 cup cherry juice
1 cup water
1/4 teasp. almond extract flavoring
3 - 4 drops red food coloring

Cake:
Cream shortening; add sugar gradually and continue beating until fluffy. Blend in eggs, beating thoroughly.

Sift flour, baking powder, baking soda and salt together; stir into creamed mixture alternately with milk.

Thoroughly drain cherries, reserving juice. Fold in cherries and nuts. Pour into greased 9 x 13-inch pan. Bake at 350 degrees for about 45 minutes.

Hot Cherry Sauce:
In a saucepan, mix sugar, cornstarch and salt; blend in juice and water. Bring to boil, stirring constantly; cook until mixture thickens and starch taste disappears (5 - 10 minutes). Remove from heat; stir in almond flavoring and red food coloring. Serve with cake.

Special Tips...

To keep a cherry cake from drying out, attach slices of bread with toothpicks to any exposed cut edges of the cake.

To ice a many layered cherry cake, try attaching all the layers with a few pieces of dry spaghetti.

When measuring flour for a cherry pie crust, always sift the flour first for a more accurate measurement.

COUNTRY CHERRY CAKE

Cake:
1 1/4 cups boiling water
1 cup quick cooking rolled oats
1/2 cup butter or margarine
1 cup sugar
1 cup brown sugar
1 teaspoon vanilla
2 eggs
1 1/2 cups flour
1 teaspoon baking soda
3/4 teaspoon cinnamon
1/2 teaspoon salt
1/4 teaspoon nutmeg

Cherry Sauce:
1/2 cup sugar
1 1/2 tablespoons cornstarch
1 (16-ounce) can tart cherries
Red food coloring, optional

Custard Sauce:
3 egg yolks
3 tablespoons sugar
1 1/2 cups milk

Cake:
Pour boiling water over rolled oats and let stand 20 minutes, stirring occasionally. Cream butter; gradually add the two sugars, creaming until smooth. Add vanilla. Beat in eggs, one at a time. Add oats and sifted dry ingredients; mix well. Pour into a greased and floured 9-inch square pan. Bake at 350 degrees for 50 - 55 minutes.

Cherry Sauce:
Combine sugar and cornstarch in saucepan; add cherries. Cook, stirring constantly until mixture is thick and clear. Add red food coloring, if desired. Cool.

Custard Sauce:
Beat egg yolks in heavy saucepan; add sugar. Gradually add 1 1/2 cups milk, stirring constantly. Cook over low heat, stirring constantly, until mixture coats a metal spoon. Remove from heat and cool at once over cold water.

To serve, cut cake into squares, top with cherries and custard sauce or whipped cream.

SAUCES

Cherry Tomato Sauce

Cherry Chutney

Sweet Cherry & Hot Pepper Glaze

Maple Cherry Sauce

Cherry Peach Conserve

Enticing Recipes for Sauces
and Preserves...

CHERRY TOMATO SAUCE

2 cups individually quick frozen tart cherries or 1 can (16 ounces) tart cherries, drained
1/2 cup cherry jelly or cherry preserves
1 bottle (12-ounces) chili sauce
1 can (10 3/4-ounces) condensed cream of tomato soup, undiluted
1 can (15-once) tomatoe sauce
In a medium saucepan, combine cherries and cherry jelly. Cook over medium heat 5 minutes. Stir in chili sauce, tomato sauce and tomato soup. Cook over low neat until sauce is hot. Pour over meatballs.

CHERRY CHUTNEY

This sauce is low-fat.

3 cups individually quick frozen tart cherries, thawed and drained
1 cup golden raisins
1 cup granulated sugar 3/4 cup vinegar
1/2 teaspoon ground cinnamon
1/2 teaspoon ground ginger
1/2 teaspoon salt
1/2 teaspoon cayenne pepper

In heavy Dutch oven, combine cherries, raisins, sugar, vinegar, walnuts, cinnamon, ginger, salt and cayenne; mix well. Bring mixture to a boil over high heat. lower heat to medium. Cook, stirring constantly, 30 to 40 minutes, or until liquid evaporates and mixture thickens.

For an appetizer, spread over cream cheese. Serve with crackers or melba toast. Equally delicious served as a relish with pork or chicken entrees. Store in tightly covered container in the refrigerator. Makes about 3 cups.

Note: If available, pitted fresh tart cherries can be used in place of frozen cherries.

> ### *How 'Bout A Few More Notes Of Interest...*
>
> *Always cut a cake from the center, then you can slide the remains next to each other to keep it fresher.*
>
> *Dried cherries are called "chaisins."*

CHERRY MAPLE SYRUP

1 can (21-ounces) cherry filling and topping
1 cup maple-flavored syrup
1/3 cup butter or margarine

In an electric blender or food processor, purée cherry filling until smooth. Pour filling into a 1 quart microwave-safe bowl. Add syrup; mix well.

Cut butter into small pieces; add to filling. Microwave, uncovered, on HIGH (100% power) 3 to 4 minutes (stirring twice, or until butter is melted and mixture is hot).

Serve over pancakes, waffles or French toast.

Makes 3 cups.

MAPLE CHERRY SAUCE

Just right for roast chicken, game birds and, of course, that holiday turkey or goose.

1 medium orange
1 can (16 ounces) tart cherries, drained, or 1 1/2 cups frozen tart cherries
1 cup maple syrup
1 cup cherry juice blend or apple-cherry juice
1/2 cup coarsely chopped walnuts, optional

Rinse orange; remove any blemishes from rind. Grate rind until you have about 1/3 cup. Same remaining orange for another use.

In a large saucepan, combine grated orange rind, cherries, maple syrup and juice. Cover and bring mixture to a rolling boil, then lower heat and simmer 10 minutes to blend flavors. Remove from heat and stir in walnuts, if desired. Cool, then cover and refrigerate. Sauce will keep 3 to 4 days; reheat before serving.

Makes 12 servings.

Note: *Nutritional information per serving without walnuts:* 103 calories, .08 grams total fat, 0 mg cholesterol, 4 mg sodium.

MAPLE CHERRY SAUCE II

Flavored with maple and orange, this sauce is terrific with roasted or grilled meats.

1/3 cup cherry juice blend
2 tablespoons cornstarch
1 cup frozen unsweetened tart cherries, thawed and well-drained
3/4 cup maple-flavored syrup
1/2 cup chopped walnuts
1 teaspoon grated orange peel

In a medium saucepan, combine cherry juice blend and cornstarch; mix well. Cook over medium heat until thickened. Add cherries, syrup, walnuts and orange peel; mix well. Cook, stirring frequently, over low heat until all ingredients are hot.

Makes 1 1/2 cups.

Serving size: 1/4 cup, 187 calories per serving. Total fat per serving: 6 grams.

SWEET CHERRY AND HOT PEPPER GLAZE

A tasty treat you have to try to believe!

1 can (16 ounces) dark sweet cherries
2 whole pickled hot yellow peppers, seeded
 and finely chopped
1/4 cup granulated sugar
2 tablespoons cornstarch

Drain cherries, reserving juice. Chop cherries. In a medium bowl, combine cherries and peppers; mix well. Set aside.

In a medium saucepan, combine sugar and cornstarch; mix well. Add enough water to reserved cherry juice to make 1 cup; gradually stir cherry juice into sugar mixture. Cook, stirring, over medium heat until thickened and bubbly. Add cherry pepper mixture; reduce heat and simmer 10 to 15 minutes. Use as a glaze on smoked chicken breasts, roasts, duck or baked ham.

Makes about 2 cups.

Serving size: 1/4 cup, 80 calories per serving. Total fat per serving: Less than 1 gram.

NO-COOK CHERRY JAM

Homemade jam tastes great on breads and rolls.

2 cups frozen unsweetened tart cherries
4 cups granulated sugar
1 pouch (3-ounces) liquid fruit pectin 1/4 cup lemon juice

Rinse clean plastic containers and lids with boiling water. Set aside.

Coarsely chop cherries while frozen. Let cherries thaw and drain.

In a large mixing bowl, combine drained cherries and sugar; mix well. Set aside for 10 minutes, stirring occasionally. In a small bowl, combine liquid fruit pectin and lemon juice; mix well. Stir pectin mixture into cherry mixture. Stir constantly 3 minutes. (A few sugar crystals may remain.)

Fill containers to within 1/2 inch of tops. Wipe off top edges of containers; quickly cover with lids. Let stand at room temperature 24 hours, then place in freezer. After opening, store in refrigerator.

Makes 4 (8-ounce) containers.

Serving size: 2 tablespoons, 13 calories per serving. Total fat per serving: Less than 1 gram.

CHERRY PRESERVES

4 1/2 cups tart cherries
5 1/2 cups sugar
4 ounces (1/2 bottle) liquid pectin
Juice of 1 lemon

Combine fruit and 1 1/2 cups of sugar; bring to a boil. Add remaining sugar, 1 cup at a time, bringing to a boil after each addition. With the last cup of sugar, add pectin and lemon juice. Cook, using candy thermometer, until temperature reaches 220 to 222 degrees. This takes 3 to 4 minutes. Do not cook more than 10 minutes. Remove from heat and cool to 190 - 200 degrees. Pour into hot sterilized jars. Seal immediately.

BLACK SWEET CHERRY CONSERVE

4 cups fresh, dark sweet cherries
3 tablespoons grated orange rind

1/4 cup lemon juice
6 cups sugar

1/2 pound chopped seedless raisins
1 teaspoon finely chopped crystalized ginger, optional
1 cup chopped nuts
1 bottle liquid pectin

Wash, stem, dry and pit cherries. Chop fine and measure 4 cups into large kettle. Add all the remaining ingredients *except the pectin*. Mix well. Over high heat, bring to a full rolling boil hard 1 minute, stirring constantly. Remove from heat and stir in pectin immediately. Skim off foam. Stir and skim alternately for five minutes. Ladle into hot, sterilized jars. Seal with paraffin or two-piece lids.

CHERRY-PEACH CONSERVE

4 cups chopped peaches
1/4 cup chopped maraschino cherries
2 tablespoons lemon juice
1 box powdered pectin
5 1/2 cups sugar

Combine peaches, cherries, lemon juice and pectin in saucepan. Bring to boil over high heat; add sugar. Bring to a full rolling boil 1 minute stirring constantly. Remove from heat. Stir and skim for 5 minutes. Ladle into hot glasses; seal with paraffin or 2 piece metal lids.

Makes about 7 cups.

CHERRY RELISH

This relish is low in fat.

3 cups fresh tart cherries
1/4 cup vinegar
1 teaspoon ground cinnamon

1 teaspoon ground cloves
1 teaspoon allspice
1 box powered pectin
4 cups sugar

Wash, pit and chop cherries. Stir in vinegar and spices; add pectin. Bring to a boil, stirring constantly. Add sugar. Return to a full rolling boil, stirring constantly; boil 1 minute. Remove from heat. Alternately stir and skim off foam for 5 minutes. Ladle into hot, sterilized jars; seal with paraffin of two piece metal lids. Serve as a meat accompaniment.

OLIVE CHERRIES

This dish is both low in fat and in calories.

2 quarts fresh dark sweet cherries
2 tablespoons canning salt
1 cup white distilled vinegar
1/4 cup sugar

Wash cherries, but do not remove stems. Pack in 4 hot pint jars. Combine remaining ingredients; bring to a boil and pour over cherries, dividing equally in jars; fill to top with cold water. Process in boiling water bath 10 minutes. Let stand 4 weeks before using.

PICKLED CHERRIES

These cherries are also low in fat and calories.

1 1/2 cups water	1 teaspoon mustard seed
1/2 cup vinegar	1/2 teaspoon whole allspice
1/4 cup sugar	1/2 teaspoon salt
1-inch stick cinnamon, broken up	1/4 teaspoon whole cloves
	1 quart fresh tart cherries with stems

In a saucepan, combine water, vinegar, sugar, cinnamon, mustard seed, allspice, salt and cloves. Bring to boil; simmer 8 minutes. Wash cherries, do not remove stems or pits. Pack in 2 hot pint jars, leaving 3/4-inch headspace. Pour boiling liquid over cherries. Adjust lids. Process 10 minutes in boiling water bath. Let stand at least 1 week. Drain before serving.

Makes 2 pints.

GINGER SPICED CHERRIES

1 (16-ounce) can dark sweet cherries
1 tablespoon cornstarch
2 teaspoons lemon juice
2 tablespoons sugar
1 tablespoon candied ginger, thinly sliced

Drain cherries, reserving juice; add water if needed to make 1 cup liquid. Mix a small amount of cherry juice and cornstarch. Combine with the rest of the cherry juice, lemon juice, sugar and ginger. Cook until clear and thick; add cherries. Serve cold as meat accompaniment.

MARASCHINO CHERRY CHUTNEY

1 (10-ounce) jar maraschino cherries
1 (10-ounce) package frozen peach slices, thawed (3/4 cup)
1/2 cup chopped walnuts
1 tablespoon finely chopped preserved ginger
2 tablespoons honey

Cut maraschino cherries in quarters; drain well. Cut peaches into pieces, drain. Mix all ingredients in saucepan. Cover and cook over low heat 8 to 10 minutes, stirring occasionally. Cool. Serve as a curry accompaniment.

Makes about 3 cups.

CURRIED FRUIT

1 (29-ounce) can pear halves, drained
4 ounces red maraschino cherries, drained
1 (29-ounce) can peach halves, drained
4 ounces green maraschino cherries, drained
1 (20-ounce) can pineapple chunks, drained
1/3 cup butter or margarine
1 (29-ounce) can apricot halves, drained
3/4 cup brown sugar

1 teaspoon curry powder

Combine pears, peaches, pineapple, apricots and cherries in a three quart casserole. Melt butter; blend in sugar and curry powder; spread over fruit. Bake 350 degrees for 30 minutes. Serve warm as an accompaniment with ham or chicken.

CHOCOLATE CHERRY CLUSTERS

1 cup semi-sweet chocolate chips   1 tablespoon water
3 tablespoons light corn syrup   1/2 cup dried cherries

Melt chocolate chips with corn syrup and water. Stir to blend. Fold in cherries. Drop by teaspoonsful on waxed paper. Cool.

Makes about 20 pieces.

CHOCOLATE DIPPED CHERRIES

8 ounces semi-sweet chocolate bits
1 tablespoon orange extract
48 dark sweet cherries, well-drained

Heat the chocolate over hot water until partly melted. Remove from heat; add extract and stir rapidly until entirely melted. Leave over warm water while dipping. Using a toothpick, dip the cherries in the chocolate. Put on waxed paper to harden. Refrigerate before serving.

NO-COOK CHERRY DIVINITY

1 (7.2-ounce) box fluffy white frosting mix
1/3 cup light corn syrup
1 teaspoon vanilla

1 pound confectioner's sugar
1/2 cup chopped maraschino cherries
1/2 cup pecans

Combine frosting mix (dry), corn syrup, vanilla and boiling water in mixing bowl. Beat on high speed until stiff peaks form, about 5 minutes. On low speed or by hand, gradually blend in sugar. Stir in cherries and nuts.

Drop mixture by teaspoons onto waxed paper. When outside of candy feels firm, turn over and allow to dry at least 12 hours. Store candy in airtight container. Can be frozen up to 2 months.

CHERRY DIVINITY

2 1/3 cups sugar
1/4 teaspoon salt
2/3 cup light corn syrup
1/2 cup water
2 egg whites, stiffly beaten
1 teaspoon vanilla
Red food coloring
1 cup sliced candied or maraschino cherries

In saucepan, combine sugar, salt, corn syrup and water. Cook, stirring constantly, until sugar dissolves and mixture boils. Continue cooking, without stirring, until small amount of syrup forms hard ball in cold water (265 degrees), wiping away crystals from sides of pan with damp cloth.

Pour slowly over egg whites, beating constantly, and continue beating until candy hold its shape when dripped from spoon; mix in vanilla and a little red food coloring to tint candy a delicate pink. Add cherries. Drop by teaspoons onto a buttered surface. Makes about 36 pieces.

CHERRY-CHOCOLATE CREAMS

1 cup semi-sweet chocolate bits

1/3 cup evaporated milk
1 1/2 cups sifted powdered sugar
2/3 cup finely chopped maraschino cherries

1/2 cup finely chopped walnuts
1 cup flaked coconut
Red food coloring

Melt chocolate bits and milk together over low heat, stirring constantly. Gradually blend in powdered sugar. Add cherries and nuts. Chill until mixture is stiff enough to handle. Toss food coloring with the coconut to tint pink. Shape dough into 1 inch balls and roll in coconut. Chill. Ripen 2 days in the refrigerator.

Makes about 4 dozen.

WHITE FRUITED FUDGE

2 cups sugar
1 cup half & half
1/4 cup butter or margarine
1/4 cup light corn syrup
cherries

1 teaspoon vanilla
1/2 cup coarsely chopped nuts
1/3 cup chopped red candied cherries
1/3 cup chopped green candied

Combine sugar, half & half, butter, corn syrup, and salt in large heavy saucepan. Bring to gentle boil over low heat. Cook, stirring constantly, until sugar melts. Continue cooking stirring occasionally until mixture reaches the soft-ball stage (283-240 degrees).

Remove from heat. Stir in marshmallows and vanilla; stir until marshmallows melt and candy starts to lose its gloss.

Stir in nuts and fruit; stir until candy starts to set. Pour into buttered 8-inch square pan. Cool; score in squares while still slightly warm.

To Make Baking Easier...

Always use unsalted butter when greasing a pan; chances of having a sticking problem will be greatly reduced.

To make a delicate cherry cake, use half unbleached white flour and half whole wheat flour.

A teaspoon of vinegar added to the pie dough will guarantee a flaky crust.

BEVERAGES

Festive Cherry Punch

Cherry Slush

Cherry Bounce

Jingle Bell Punch

Thirst Quenching, Simply
Outrageous Beverages...

FESTIVE CHERRY PUNCH

Bowl 'em over with this party beverage.

4 cups cherry juice blend, chilled
1 bottle (1 liter) ginger ale, chilled
Ice ring (instructions follow)

Just before serving, combine cherry juice blend and ginger ale in a large punch bowl. Add ice ring.

For decorative ice ring: Place a ring mold or other decorative mold in freezer; let chill. Rinse inside of mold with cold water; return to freezer until thin coating of ice forms. Cover the bottom of the mold in a decorative pattern with maraschino cherries. Gently add enough cherry juice blend to just cover fruit. Freeze until firm. Gently add more cherry juice blend to fill mold completely. Freeze overnight, or until firm.

Makes about 16 servings.
Serving size: 1/2 cup, 53 calories per serving. Total fat per serving: 0 grams.

CHERRY SLUSH

Quench your thirst with an icy sparkler.

2 cups cherry juice blend or water
1 cup granulated sugar
2 cups frozen unsweetened tart cherries
1 can (6 ounces) frozen orange juice
1 bottle (2 liters) lemon-lime carbonated beverage, chilled

In a medium saucepan, combine cherry juice blend and sugar. Cook over medium heat, stirring frequently, until sugar dissolves and mixture boils. Reduce heat; simmer 3 minutes. Remove from heat.

In electric blender or food processor container, combine cherries, orange juice concentrate and lemon juice. Blend 1 minute, or until cherries are puréed. In a 6 cup freezer container, combine cherry mixture and sugar mixture; mix well. Cover tightly; freeze 5 hours or overnight. Remove cherry mixture from freezer 30 minutes before serving. Put 1/4 cup slush in each glass; add 1/2 cup carbonated beverage to each glass. Serve immediately. Freeze remaining slush for later use. Makes 16 servings.

Note: 1 can (16 ounces) unsweetened tart cherries, drained, can be substituted for frozen cherries.

Serving size: 3/4 cup, 109 calories per serving. Total fat per serving: less than 1 gram.

HOLLYBERRY PUNCH

1 (6-ounce) can frozen lemonade concentrate
1 (6-ounce) can frozen orange juice concentrate
5 cups water
2/3 cup maraschino cherry juice
1 (28-ounce) bottle ginger ale

Combine juices, water and maraschino cherry juice; mix well. Add ginger ale. Pour over ice in punch bowl. Float slices of lemon and/or orange for garnish, if desired. Makes about 20 four-ounce servings.

JINGLE BELL PUNCH

2 quarts cranberry juice, chilled
1 (6-ounce) can frozen lemonade concentrate, thawed
1/2 cup maraschino cherry juice
42 ounces carbonated lemon-lime beverage, chilled

Combine all ingredients except lemon-lime beverage. At serving time, pour over ice in a punch bowl. Add lemon-lime beverage. Individual servings can be garnished with lemon slice, orange wedge and maraschino cherry, alternated on cocktail picks.

Makes about 30 four-ounce servings.

CHERRY BOUNCE

1 quart fresh sweet cherries
1/2 pound sugar cubes
1 tablespoon whole allspice
1 tablespoon whole cinnamon
1 tablespoon whole cloves
1 pint whiskey

Wash cherries and pick off the stems. Fill a large-mouthed bottle alternately with a thick layer of cherries, a layer of sugar, and a few of the whole spices. Repeat until the bottle is almost full. Add whiskey to fill. Cork and let stand in a dark place for 2 months or more. The older it is, the better. Strain before serving as a liqueur. Serve the cherries as hors d'oeuvres.

CHERRY-COLA SODA, BLENDER STYLE

3/4 cup cold cola beverage
1/2 cup sugar
2 cups dark sweet cherries
4 large scoops vanilla ice cream
Cola beverage

In electric blender jar, mix 3/4 cup cola and sugar. Add cherries and ice cream; blend until thick and smooth. Divide mixture between 8 tall glasses. Fill with cola beverage. Give a quick stir and top each with a scoop of ice cream.

MERRY CHERRY PUNCH

2 (3.3-ounce) packages pre-sweetened cherry soft drink mix
2 cups cherry juice
2 (46-ounce) cans cherry drink
2 (28-ounce) bottles ginger ale
2 trays ice cubes, with stemmed maraschino cherries frozen into each cube

Combine all ingredients with ice cubes in chilled bowl.

CHERRY-APPLE PUNCH

1 quart apple juice
1 quart cherry drink
1 (6-ounce) can frozen lemonade concentrate, thawed
1/2 cup maraschino cherry juice
24 ounces carbonated lemon-lime beverage, chilled
24 ounces carbonated wild cherry beverage, chilled

Combine all ingredients, except carbonated beverages. At serving time, pour over ice in a punch bowl. Add lemon-lime and wild cherry beverages. Garnish with apple or orange wedges and stemmed maraschino cherry alternated on cocktail picks, if desired.

Makes about 30 four-ounce servings.

DIPS

Dried Cherry Relish

Veggie Dip

*Great Dips, Full of
Flavor and Zest...*

VEGGIE DIP

A dressed up dip for your next party.

1 cup chopped dried tart cherries
1/2 cup crumbled blue cheese (about 2 ounces)
1/2 cup chopped walnuts
1 cup Lite sour cream
1/4 cup mayonnaise

In a medium bowl, combine cherries, blue cheese and walnuts. Stir in sour cream and mayonnaise; mix well. Chill about 1 hour to blend flavors. Serve with vegetable dippers, such as celery, carrots, cauliflower, cucumber, broccoli, green or red bell peppers.

Makes 2 cups dip.

Serving size: 2 tablespoons, 113 calories per serving. Total fat per serving: 8 grams.

DRIED CHERRY RELISH

Serve warm with pork, duck or goose.

1 1/2 cups dried tart cherries
1/2 cup red wine vinegar
1/4 cup balsamic vinegar
1 tablespoon butter or margarine
1 large red onion, finely chopped
2 tablespoons granulated sugar
1/4 teaspoon salt, or to taste
1/8 teaspoon ground black pepper

In a medium bowl, combine cherries, red wine vinegar and balsamic vinegar. Let soak 30 minutes.

Heat butter in a large skillet. Add onion; cook 5 minutes, or until onion is soft. Add sugar; mix well. Cook, stirring occasionally, over low heat 10 minutes.

Add cherries with soaking liquid to onion mixture. Simmer, uncovered, 10 to 15 minutes, or until almost all the liquid is evaporated. Season with salt and pepper. Serve warm.

Makes about 2 cups; 12 servings as a relish.

Note: Relish may be prepared ahead of time and refrigerated; reheat before serving.

Serving size: 3 tablespoons, 66 calories per serving. Total fat per serving: 1 gram

SOUPS

Two versions of

Cherry Soup

Sure To Make Your

Mouth Water...

CHERRY SOUP

Delicately flavored, this cold soup goes well with main course salads.

1/2 cup frozen unsweetened tart cherries
1/2 cup frozen dark sweet cherries
1 cup custard-style cherry low-fat yogurt
1 cup sour cream
1 cup heavy cream
1/2 cup dried tart cherries
1 tablespoon grenadine
1 tablespoon granulated sugar or to taste
1/4 teaspoon ground nutmeg

Thaw tart and sweet cherries, reserving their juice. In an electric blender or food processor container, purée tart and sweet cherries with juice until smooth. Set aside.

In a large mixing bowl, combine yogurt, sour cream, heavy cream and dried cherries; mix well. Add puréed cherries, grenadine, sugar and nutmeg; mix well. Let chill 1 to 2 hours to blend flavors. Serve chilled.

Makes 6 servings.

Serving size: 1/2 cup, 319 calories per serving. Total fat per serving: 19 grams.

CHERRY SOUP II

A Hungarian specialty.

1 quart water
2 - 2 1/2 pounds frozen sweetened tart cherries, slightly thawed
1/2 teaspoon salt
1/2 cup salt water
1/4 cup flour
3 egg yolks, slightly beaten
1 cup Lite sour cream

Boil quart water in a large saucepan. Add cherries and salt. Return to boiling; simmer, covered, 10 minutes. Pour the 1/2 cup cold water into a 1-pint screw-top jar. Add flour; cover jar tightly; shake until blended. Stirring constantly, slowly pour flour mixture into hot cherry mixture; bring to boiling, and cook 2 to 3 minutes. Remove from heat; gradually add 1/3 cup hot soup to the egg yolks, stirring vigorously; blend into soup. Stirring constantly, cook over low heat 3 to 5 minutes (do not boil). Remove from heat. Gradually add 1 cup hot soup to the sour cream, stirring vigorously; blend into remaining soup. Chill and serve cold, or serve hot, if desired. Makes 8 to 10 servings.

SIDE DISHES

Acorn Squash with Cherries

Red Currant-Cherry Jam

Yams on the Half Shell

Dried Cherries

Cherry Cinnamon Sauce

Fantastic Side Dishes...

ACORN SQUASH WITH CHERRIES

This dish is also lowfat and low in calories.

2 acorn squash (about 3 pounds total)
1 can (21 ounces) cherry filling and topping
1/2 teaspoon ground cinnamon
1/4 teaspoon ground ginger
1 tablespoon butter or margarine
Salt and ground black pepper (optional)

Cut squash in half lengthwise and remove seeds. Place squash, hollow side up, on large, microwave-safe dish, with stem ends to the outside of dish. Cover with plastic wrap. Microwave on HIGH (100% power) 5 minutes; rotate dish 1/4 turn. Microwave 2 minutes on HIGH.

In a medium bowl, combine cherry filling, cinnamon and ginger; mix well.

Divide butter into 4 equal parts and put in the bottom of each acorn cavity. Season with salt and pepper, if desired.

Fill acorn cavities with equal portions of cherry mixture. Microwave, uncovered, on HIGH 3 to 5 minutes (turning once), or until cherries are hot.

Makes 4 servings.

Be Prepared To Cook With These Helpful Tips...

To maintain the shape of a cherry souffle, serve immediately after it is steam baked and always on a warm plate.

If you bake a cherry angel food cake on the bottom rack at 325 degrees, you will make a moister cake.

Adding 1/4 teaspoon of almond extract to cherry or peach pies will give them a better flavor.

For a flakier pastry shell or pie crust, add 1 teaspoon or lemon juice to the batter.

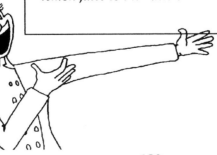

ACORN SQUASH

Salt and black pepper, to taste
1/2 cup dried tart cherries
1 tablespoon slivered almonds
3 tablespoons cherry preserves
2 teaspoons water
1/4 teaspoon ground cinnamon

Cut squash in half lengthwise and remove seeds. Place squash cut-side down, in a microwave-safe dish, with stem ends to the outside of dish. Cover with plastic wrap. Microwave on HIGH (100% power) 5 minutes. Rotate dish one-quarter turn. Microwave 2 minutes on HIGH. Remove squash from microwave and carefully remove plastic wrap. Season with salt and pepper.

In a small bowl, combine cherries and almonds. Divide mixture evenly between squash cavities. In the same bowl, combine preserves, water and cinnamon; mix well. Top cherry filling with equal portions of preserves mixture. Microwave, uncovered, on HIGH 3 to 5 minutes, or until cherry mixture is hot, rotating dish once.

Note: For conventional cooking, place squash halves, cut-side down, in a vegetable steamer. Place steamer over boiling water in a large pan. Steam, covered, 15 minutes, or until squash is crisp-tender. Fill squash as directed above. Steam, covered, 5 minutes, or until cherry mixture is hot. Makes 2 servings.

Serving size: 1/2 squash, 247 calories per serving. Total fat per serving; 2 grams.

YAMS ON THE HALF SHELL

4 medium yams or sweet potatoes
2 tablespoons butter or margarine
3/4 cup thick cherry preserves
1 teaspoon nutmeg
1/4 cup chopped pecans

Bake yams or sweet potatoes at 375 degrees just until done, about 40 to 45 minutes. With sharp knife, slice off top 1/3 of each potato, lengthwise. Scoop pulp from bottoms, leaving 1/8 inch layer of potato next to skin. Mash the yam or sweet potato pulp until free of lumps. Stir in butter or margarine, 1/2 cup of the preserves and nutmeg; beat until smooth. Stir in nuts.

Spoon mixture into hollowed-out bottom skins. Arrange on shallow pan; drizzle 1 tablespoon of preserves over top of each yam and return to 375 degree oven for about 15 minutes or until heated through. Note: may use 350 degree oven and increase baking time to 45 to 60 minutes and reheating time to 20 to 25 minutes.

Variation:
1 (17-ounce) can vacuum packed sweet potatoes
1 1/2 tablespoons butter or margarine
1/2 cup thick cherry preserves
3/4 teaspoons nutmeg
1/4 cup chopped pecans

Heat and mash sweet potatoes. Mix in remaining ingredients until smooth, reserving 1/2 of preserves. Pour mixture into shallow 1 quart casserole. Drizzle remaining preserves over top. Bake at 350 degrees for 25 to 30 minutes, or until hot.

Makes 4 servings.

DRIED CHERRIES

In a heavy saucepan, combine pitted tart cherries and sugar, using the proportion of one cup of sugar for each quart of pitted cherries. (See below for the sugarless method.) Red food coloring can be added as desired to give the finished product a better color.

Simmer the cherries and sugar over medium heat for 20 minutes, stirring occasionally. Drain off juice; save for other use as desired.

Spread drained cherries in a single layer on an aluminum foil lined baking sheet. Dry in a 200 degree oven for several hours; leave the oven door ajar. Stir and turn fruit occasionally. Drying time will vary considerably, depending upon the size and quantity of cherries, their degree of ripeness, and relative humidity.

Cherries are dry when they resemble raisins. Remove the cherries from the baking sheet while still warm; cool thoroughly. Store in a cool, dark, dry, place in tightly covered containers.

Dried cherries can be eaten as a snack or substituted for raisins in any recipe. This method of preparation will produce dried cherries very similar to the commercial product. If you prefer a more tart snack, simply eliminate the sugar. The pitted tart cherries can be put directly on a baking sheet and dried; drying time is not noticeably increased.

RED CURRANT-CHERRY JAM

1 1/4 quarts currant
2 1/2 pounds tart cherries
1 box powdered pectin
6 cups sugar

Crush fully ripe currants; sieve half of pulp. Pit fully ripe cherries; chop fine or grind. Measure 4 1/4 cups prepared fruit. Combine fruit and pectin in saucepan. Bring to a boil over high heat, stirring constantly; add sugar. Bring to a full rolling boil; boil 1 minute, stirring constantly. Remove from heat; skim off foam. Alternately skim and stir for 5 minutes. Ladle into hot jars; seal with 2 piece lids or paraffin. Makes 8 cups.

SWEET CHERRY CONSERVE

2 1/2 pounds dark sweet cherries
1 cup crushed pineapple, undrained
Juice and grated peel of 1 lemon

1 box powdered pectin
4 cups sugar
1/2 cup chopped nuts

Wash, pit and cut cherries into small pieces. Measure 4 cups chopped cherries into kettle with crushed pineapple. Add lemon peel and juice. Blend fruits thoroughly. On high heat, add pectin gradually, stirring constantly. Continue stirring and bring to a vigorous boil. Add sugar gradually. Add nuts; cook and stir until mixture comes to a full rolling boil. Boil for 2 minutes. Remove from heat and let mixture stand for 5 minutes with alternate stirring and skimming. Pour into hot sterilized jars and seal immediately. Yield: 6 1/2 pint jars.

CHERRY-CINNAMON SAUCE

1 (16-ounce) can tart cherries
1/2 cup sugar
2 tablespoons cornstarch
3 tablespoons red cinnamon candies
1 tablespoon lemon juice

Drain cherries, reserving liquid; add water if needed to make 1 cup liquid. Combine sugar and cornstarch in saucepan. Gradually add liquid, and cinnamon candies. Heat to a boil, stirring constantly; continue cooking until mixture is thick and clear. Remove from heat. Stir in lemon juice and cherries. Cool.

Makes about 2 1/2 cups sauce.

Use as glaze for meat, such as pork roast, or as topping for pudding or other desserts.

SPICY-CHERRY SAUCE

1 (16-ounce) can tart cherries
1 cup sugar
1/4 cup cornstarch
1/4 teaspoon salt
1/8 teaspoon ground cloves
1/8 teaspoon ground cinnamon

1/2 teaspoon lemon rind
1/4 teaspoon red food coloring
2 tablespoons lemon juice

Drain cherries, reserving juice; add water to make 2 cups liquid. In a saucepan, combine sugar, cornstarch and salt; gradually add liquid. Stir in remaining ingredients. Cook, stirring constantly, until thick and clear. Serve with meats, poultry, or desserts.

Your Cherry Recipes Will Turn Out Fabulous If You Follow These Easy Tips:

Never overcrowd your oven; heat must circulate freely around all items that are in the oven or they won't bake evenly.

To make sure that your baking powder is fresh, try pouring very hot tap water over a teaspoonful. If it's fresh it will bubble very actively.

To keep waxed paper down on the counter when rolling dough, try wetting the counter first.

Cherry pits can be pried out by using a bent paper clip.

Before baking a pie that is juicy, insert a tube of macaroni in the center of the top of the pie and the juices won't bubble out.

Low-Fat

Hot 'N' Spicy Chicken

Low-Cholesterol Cherry Dessert

Cherry Angel Pie

Cherry Salsa

*Full of Flavor, But Not
Full of Fat...*

CHERRY DESSERT

2 egg whites, beaten
1 1/2 cups granulated sugar, divided
1 teaspoon vanilla
1/4 teaspoon salt
1 teaspoon baking powder
1/2 cup all-purpose flour
1 1/2 cups frozen tart cherries, thawed (or fresh tart cherries, pitted), divided
1/2 cup chopped walnuts or pecans
2 tablespoons cornstarch
1/4 teaspoon almond extract
Whipped cream or frozen vanilla yogurt

In a large mixing bowl with an electric mixer, beat egg whites until foamy. Add 3/4 cup sugar, vanilla, salt and baking powder; beat until smooth and fluffy. Add flour; blend well. Drain juice from cherries and reserve. Stir in 1 cup drained tart cherries and chopped walnuts. Pour into a greased 8-inch pie pan. Bake in a preheated 350 degree oven 30 minutes.

Meanwhile, add enough water to reserved cherry juice to make 1 cup. In a medium saucepan, combine liquid, remaining 3/4 cup sugar and cornstarch. Cook over medium heat until thickened and bubbly. Add remaining 1/2 cup drained cherries and 1/4 teaspoon almond extract. Mix well. Keep cherry sauce warm. Cut cake into wedges. Top each serving with cherry sauce. If desired, garnish with whipped cream or frozen vanilla yogurt. Makes 6 to 8 servings.

Note: 1 can (16 ounces) tart cherries can be substituted for frozen cherries.

CHERRY ANGEL PIE

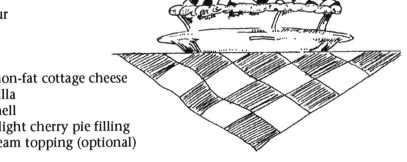

2 tablespoons flour
1/4 cup sugar
1/8 teaspoon salt
2 egg whites
2 cups lowfat or non-fat cottage cheese
1/2 teaspoon vanilla
9" unbaked pie shell
1 (20-ounce) can light cherry pie filling
Light whipped cream topping (optional)

Put egg whites and cottage cheese in blender. Blend until cottage cheese is pureed. Add sugar, salt, flour, vanilla and blend into cheese mixture. Pour into unbaked 9" pie shell. Bake at 350 degrees for 1 hour. When cool, top with one 20-ounce can light cherry pie filling. If desired add light whipped cream.

HOT 'N'SPICY CHICKEN

This is also a low calorie main course.

2 whole chicken breasts, boned and skinned
1 can (21-ounces) cherry filling and topping
2 whole, pickled Banana peppers (large, hot
  yellow peppers), seeded and finely chopped
1/2 cup chopped onion
1 teaspoon dry mustard

Cut chicken into bite size (1/2-inch) pieces. Place chicken in a single layer in an ungreased 9-inch round microwave-safe dish.

In a small bowl, combine cherry filling, peppers, onion and mustard; mix well. Pour cherry sauce over chicken. Microwave, uncovered, on HIGH (100 % power) 5 minutes. Stir mixture to break up pieces of chicken that cooked together. Microwave on HIGH 5 more minutes; stir again. Microwave on HIGH 2 to 3 minutes, or until sauce is hot and bubbly and chicken is cooked.

Serve as a main course with rice or as part of an appetizer buffet.

Makes 4 main-course servings; 10 appetizer servings.

SWEET-SOUR SHRIMP

1 can (21-ounces) cherry filling and topping
3 tablespoons cider vinegar
3 tablespoons brown sugar
1 teaspoon ground ginger
1 green pepper, seeded and cut into thin strips
1 can (8-ounces) sliced water chestnuts, well-drained
1 pound peeled and cooked medium shrimp, well-drained
Hot, cooked rice

In a 2 quart microwave-safe bowl, combine cherry filling, vinegar, brown sugar and ginger. Mix well. Stir in green pepper, water chestnuts and shrimp. Mix just to combine.

Cover bowl with waxed paper. Microwave on HIGH (100 % power) 4 to 5 minutes (stirring 2 or 3 times), or until hot.

Serve over rice.

Makes 4 servings.

CHERRY-GLAZED YAMS

1 pound cooked yams
3 ounces cherry preserves

Peel yams and slice or leave whole. Put in buttered baking dish. If sliced, spread half the preserves between layers. Drizzle remaining preserves over top. Cover and bake at 350 degrees for about 15 minutes or until heated through.

CHERRY SALSA

Served with grilled poultry, roast pork or tortilla chips. this spicy mixture wows traditional salsa lovers.

1 1/3 cup frozen unsweetened tart cherries
1/4 cup coarsely chopped dried tart cherries
1/4 cup finely chopped red onion
1 tablespoon chopped fresh or canned jalapeño peppers, or to taste
1 clove garlic, minced
1/4 teaspoon dried cilantro
1 teaspoon cornstarch

Coarsely chop frozen tart cherries. Let cherries thaw and drain, reserving 1 tablespoon cherry juice.

Combine drained cherries, dried cherries, onion, jalapeños, garlic and cilantro in a medium saucepan; mix well. In a small container, combine reserved cherry juice and cornstarch; mix until smooth, then stir into cherry mixture. Cook, stirring constantly, over medium-high heat until mixture is thickened. Let cool.

Makes about 1 cup.

Serving size: 2 tablespoons; 25 calories per serving. Total fat per serving: Less than 1 gram

CHERRY DELIGHT

Colorful addition to potluck suppers.

1 can (21-ounces) cherry filling and topping
1 container (16-ounces) lowfat cottage cheese
1/2 cup slivered almonds
1/2 teaspoon almond extract, or to taste
1 cup frozen whipped topping, thawed
Fresh mint leaves.

In a large mixing bowl, combine cherry filling, cottage cheese, almonds and almond extract; mix well. Fold in whipped topping. Let chill until ready to serve. Garnish with mint leaves, if desired. Serve as a salad, dessert or snack.

Makes 6 servings.

Serving size: 1/2 cup, 165 calories per cup. Total fat per serving: 6 grams.

GLORIFIED RICE

1 cup whipped dessert topping
1/2 teaspoon almond extract
Red food coloring
1 (16-ounce) can dark sweet cherries, drained
1 (20-ounce) can crushed pineapple, drained
2 cups cooked rice, chilled
1 1/3 cups small marshmallows

Combine dessert topping, extract and a few drops red food coloring. Fold in remaining ingredients. Chill two or three hours before serving.

Chef Secrets To Help You Out...

If you must cut a cherry cake while its still hot, use a piece of unwaxed dental floss, instead of a knife.

To prevent a soggy crust on a pastry shell, try coating the shell with egg white before baking.

EAST INDIAN RICE SALAD

Savory salad provides fruit and fiber.

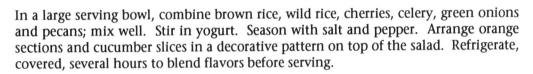

2 cups cooked brown rice
1 cup cooked wild rice
1 cup dried tart cherries
1/4 cup thinly sliced celery
1/4 cup thinly sliced green onions
1/4 cup chopped pecans
1/4 to 1/2 cup plain lowfat yogurt, to taste
Salt and pepper, to taste
1 can (11-ounces) mandarin oranges, drained
1/2 cucumber, peeled, halved lengthwise, seeded and sliced

In a large serving bowl, combine brown rice, wild rice, cherries, celery, green onions and pecans; mix well. Stir in yogurt. Season with salt and pepper. Arrange orange sections and cucumber slices in a decorative pattern on top of the salad. Refrigerate, covered, several hours to blend flavors before serving.

Makes 8 servings.

Serving size: 3/4 cup, 164 calories per serving. Total fat per serving: 3 grams

WALDORF SALAD

1 cup finely chopped celery
1 cup chopped red apples
 1 cup canned light cherries, drained
1 cup canned mandarin oranges, drained
1 banana, sliced
1/2 cup chopped nuts
1/4 cup Lite sour cream
1/4 cup Lite mayonnaise or Lite-salad dressing
1/2 teaspoon honey

Combine celery, fruits and nuts. Mix sour cream, mayonnaise and honey together. Fold into fruit mixture.

Serve chilled on lettuce leaf or in lettuce-lined bowl.

CHERRY BARS

A great pick-me-up any time of day.

3/4 cup butter or margarine
2 cups firmly packed brown sugar
2 cups all-purpose flour
2 cups old-fashioned or quick-cooking oats, uncooked
2 teaspoons baking soda
1 can (21-ounces) cherry filling and topping
2 tablespoons granulated sugar
1 tablespoon cornstarch
1/2 teaspoon almond extract

In a mixing bowl with an electric mixer, beat butter and brown sugar until light and fluffy. Combine flour, oats and baking soda. Add flour mixture to sugar mixture; mix on low speed until crumbly. Spread two-thirds of the oat mixture into the bottom of an ungreased 13 x 9 x 2-inch baking pan. Press down to make a firm layer.

In an electric blender or food processor container, purée cherry filling until smooth. Pour puréed cherry filling into a medium saucepan. Combine granulated sugar and cornstarch; stir into cherry filling. Cook, stirring constantly, over low heat until mixture is thick and bubbly. Stir in almond extract. Pour cherry mixture over oat layer; spread evenly. Top with remaining oat mixture.

Bake in a preheated 325 degree oven 45 minutes, or until golden brown. Let cool before cutting.

Makes 32 bars.

Serving size 1 (2-inch) piece, 162 calories per serving. Total fat per serving: 4 1/2 grams.

CHERRY NUGGET AND CARROT SALAD

2 cups chopped or coarsely ground carrots (4 - 5 medium)
1/4 cup finely diced celery
1/2 cup (2-ounces) dried cherries (cherry nuggets)
1/2 cup Lite salad dressing or Lite mayonnaise
1/2 cup walnut or pecan pieces, optional

Toss all ingredients together until well-mixed. Serve in glass bowl, or in lettuce cups.

STUFFED HAM-CHERRY ROLL

Sauce:
1 (16-ounce) can tart cherries
1 1/2 tablespoons cornstarch
1/4 cup sugar
1/4 teaspoon allspice
1/4 teaspoon cloves
Red food coloring, optional

Stuffing:
4 cups soft bread crumbs
1/4 cup celery, finely chopped
1/2 cup onion, chopped
1/2 cup toasted almonds
1/2 teaspoon salt
1/8 teaspoon pepper
1/4 cup 2 % milk
2 pounds boneless ham, thinly sliced

Sauce:
Drain cherries, reserving juice; add water if needed to make 1 cup liquid. Add cornstarch, sugar and spices to liquid and stir thoroughly; simmer until thick and clear. Add chopped cherries and coloring.

Stuffing:
Combine all ingredients except ham. Lay 3 pieces of light twine on counter, each about 28 inches long. Overlap thin slices of ham to an 11 x 8-inch rectangle. Spread stuffing to within about one inch of the edge. Cover with cherry sauce, reserving 1/2 cup. Roll carefully and tie with twine. Bake at 350 degrees for 30 minutes. Serve warm with reserved cherry sauce.

CREAMY CHERRY MOLD

1 (16-ounce) can dark sweet cherries
1 (3-ounce) package cherry gelatin
2 cups Lite sour cream

Drain cherries, reserving juice; add water to make 2 cups liquid. Heat 1 cup of the liquid to boiling and pour over gelatin. Stir until dissolved. Stir in remaining liquid. Chill until mixture is slightly thickened, stirring occasionally. Stir in sour cream. Halve cherries and fold into gelatin mixture. Pour into oiled 1 1/2 quart mold and chill until firm. Unmold onto a chilled serving plate.

CHERRY BINGO

1 cup cola
1 (8-ounce) can crushed pineapple, drained
1 1/2 cups juice of cherries (juice from cherries, plus water to equal 1 1/2 cups)
1 (16-ounce) can dark sweet cherries, drained
1 cup pecan pieces
1 (6-ounce) package cherry gelatin
1 cup hot water

Pre-measure the first five ingredients and put in freezer several hours ahead.

Dissolve gelatin in hot water. Add the partially frozen cherry juice and stir. Add other partially frozen ingredients and mix thoroughly. Pour into 1 1/2 quart mold and refrigerate. This will set very quickly.

Makes 10 to 12 servings.

CHERRY ROYALE TARTS

1/4 cup plus 1 1/2 teaspoons sugar
1/4 teaspoon salt
1 1/2 tablespoons cornstarch
1 egg, well-beaten
1 1/2 cups 15 or skim milk
1/2 teaspoon vanilla
1/8 teaspoon almond extract
1 (21-ounce) can cherry pie filling
12 tart shells, baked

Combine sugar, salt and cornstarch; mix well. Add to egg and beat well. Scald milk, add egg mixture gradually, stirring constantly; heat until thick and bubbly, about 5 minutes. Remove from heat. Add vanilla and almond extract. Cover container with wax paper to prevent forming a "skin". Stir occasionally until completely cold. Custard will be thick.

Fill tart shells about half full with custard; top with cherry pie filling.

QUICK CHERRY PIE

1 (14-ounce) can sweetened condensed milk
1/4 cup lemon juice
1 (16-ounce) can tart cherries, drained
1/4 teaspoon almond extract
9-inch graham cracker pie crust
1/2 cup coconut

Blend condensed milk and lemon juice. Stir in cherries and almond extract; pour mixture into pie shell. Sprinkle coconut over top. Chill until ready to serve.

HONEY CHERRY COOKIES

2 cups flour
1/2 teaspoon baking soda
1/2 teaspoon salt
1/2 cup shortening
1 cup honey
1 egg
1/2 cup sour milk
3/4 cup chopped pecans
3/4 cup drained chopped tart cherries
3/4 cup dates, cut up
3/4 cup raisins

Sift together flour, soda and salt. Cream shortening and honey; add the egg, sour milk and flour mixture. Fold nuts and fruits. Drop teaspoonsful onto greased cookie sheets. Bake at 350 for 15 to 18 minutes.

Makes about 5 dozen.

FRUIT FLAMBE

1 (16-ounce) can light sweet cherries
1 (16-ounce) can apricot halves
1 (20-ounce) can pineapple chunks
1 (11-ounce) can mandarin oranges
1 cup combined reserved fruit syrups
1/2 cup brandy

Drain cherries, apricots, pineapple and oranges, reserving syrups. In saucepan, heat 1 cup reserved syrups to a boil; reduce heat to "warm". Add fruit gently and heat through.

Just before serving, heat brandy in small saucepan just until it reaches a boil. Pour over heated fruit and ignite. Serve in dessert dishes or as a sauce over ice cream or unfrosted cake slices.

HOLIDAY FRUIT COMPOTE

1 (20-ounce) can pineapple slices or chunks
1 (16-ounce) can dark sweet pitted cherries*
1 (20-ounce) can peach slices*
2 bananas, peeled and sliced diagonally
1 1/2 cups frozen whole strawberries*

Drain all fruits. Arrange pineapple slices on
bottom and around sides of 2 quart glass bowl.
Put a cherry in center of each slice of pineapple.
Layer cherries, then remaining fruits in order
listed. Garnish with coconut. Chill several
hours before serving.

Makes about 10 servings.

*Fresh fruits are even nicer.
Note: bananas and other fresh fruits may be treated with ascorbic acid (use lemon
juice, or "Fruit Fresh") to prevent darkening.

FLAMED CHERRY CAKE

1 (24-ounce) loaf pound cake
1 (21-ounce) can cherry pie filling
3 tablespoons brandy

Slice pound cake into 8 slices. Put under broiler on cookie sheet; toast on both
sides. Heat can of pie filling until hot, not boiling. Spoon over toasted pound cake
on individual dessert plates. If desired, a teaspoon of heated brandy can be put in a
small hollow on top and ignited.

Cherry Notes Of Great Importance...

*To make your cakes and cookies moist, add a teaspoon of
honey to the batter.*

*When the recipe calls for flour to be sifted, add the leavening
and salt when sifting for a better blend.*

LOW-CALORIE

Turkey with Cherry Barbecue Sauce

Hot-Shot Cherries

Cherry Glazed Chicken

And Many More...

TURKEY WITH CHERRY BARBECUE SAUCE

This main course is also lowfat.

5 pounds bone-in turkey breast
1 can (21-ounces) cherry filling and topping
2 tablespoons soy sauce
2 tablespoons cooking sherry
1/2 teaspoon ground ginger
1/2 teaspoon ground allspice

Prepare grill for cooking using indirect heat method with drip pan in the center of coals. Place turkey breast, breast-side down, in a large microwave-safe dish. Cover with plastic wrap, venting one edge. Microwave on HIGH (100% power) 20 minutes, turning dish halfway through cooking time. Remove and place breast, breast-side up, on grill over drip pan. Cover grill and cook 35 to 45 minutes.

Meanwhile, in a medium microwave-safe bowl, combine cherry filling, soy sauce, sherry, ginger and allspice; mix well. Microwave on HIGH 2 to 3 minutes, stirring sauce and turning dish halfway through cooking time.

Purée 1/2 cup cherry sauce in an electric blender. Brush puréed mixture over turkey during the last 10 minutes of grilling. Keep remaining whole cherry sauce warm. Allow turkey breast to stand 15 minutes before carving. Arrange slices on serving platter and top with remaining warm cherry sauce. Makes 6 to 8 servings.

CHEERY CHERRY PASTA SALAD

This salad is low in fat.

2 cups uncooked rotini (macaroni twists)
1 cup dried cherries
1 cup diced cucumber
1/2 cup grated carrot
3 green onions, chopped
1/2 cup low-calorie mayonnaise-type salad dressings
1 tablespoon lemon juice
1 teaspoon dried dill weed
1/8 teaspoon ground black pepper, or to taste

Cook rotini according to package directions. Drain and rinse in cold water; drain well. In a large mixing bowl, combine cooked rotini, cherries, cucumber, carrot and onion; mix well. In a small bowl, combine salad dressing, lemon juice, dill and black pepper. Pour dressing over pasta mixture, tossing to coat. Cover and refrigerate 1 to 2 hours, or overnight. Makes about 5 cups; 8 servings.

Note: *Nutritional information per serving:* 168 calories, 2 grams total fat, 7.5 mg cholesterol, 23 mg sodium.

HOT SHOT CHERRIES

Pecans and cherries pack a punch!

2 cups pecan halves
1 cup dried tart cherries
2 tablespoons Worcestershire sauce
1/2 to 1 teaspoon cayenne pepper, or to taste
1/2 teaspoon garlic powder
1/2 to 1 teaspoon seasoned salt, or to taste
1/2 teaspoon cumin
1/8 teaspoon oregano
2 tablespoons, vegetable oil

In a medium bowl, combine pecans and cherries. In a small bowl, combine Worcestershire sauce, cayenne, garlic powder, seasoned salt, cumin and oregano; mix well. Pour over pecan mixture; stir to coat.

Heat oil in a large skillet over medium heat. Add pecan mixture. Cook, stirring constantly, about 5 minutes. Do not allow mixture to burn. Remove from heat. Spread pecans on waxed paper to cool. Store in a tightly covered container.

Makes about 3 cups.
Serving size: 1/4 cup, 85 calories per serving. Total fat per serving: 7 grams

HAM SPIRALS

Cherries and pecans add crunch to filling.

1 package (3 ounces) lite cream cheese, softened
1/4 cup finely chopped dried tart cherries
3 tablespoons finely chopped pecans
2 tablespoons Lite mayonnaise
1/2 teaspoon honey mustard or spicy brown mustard
4 thin slices cooked ham

In a small bowl, combine cream cheese, dried cherries, pecans, mayonnaise and mustard; mix well.

Spread cherry mixture evenly on ham slices. Roll up jelly-roll style; fasten with wooden picks. Let chill several hours. Remove wooden picks. Slice each ham roll crosswise into 1/4 inch slices; serve on crackers.

Makes about 40 (1/4 inch) pieces.
Serving size: 2 pieces, 46 calories per serving. Total fat per serving: 4 grams.

CHERRY-GLAZED CHICKEN

Yellow mustard is the secret ingredient in this recipe.

1 (2 1/2 to 3 pound) broiler-fryer chicken, cut up (or 6 chicken breasts halves, skinned and boned)

1/2 cup milk
1/2 cup all-purpose flour
1 teaspoon dried thyme
Salt and pepper, to taste
1 to 2 tablespoons vegetable oil
1 can (16 ounces) unsweetened tart cherries
1/4 cup brown sugar
1/4 granulated sugar
1 teaspoon prepared yellow mustard

Rinse chicken; pat dry with paper towels. Pour milk into a shallow container. In another container, combine flour, thyme, salt and pepper. Dip chicken first in milk, then in flour mixture; coat evenly.

Heat oil in skillet. Add chicken; brown on all sides. Put chicken in a 13 x 9 x 2-inch baking dish. Bake, covered with aluminum foil, in a preheated 350 degree oven 30 minutes

Meanwhile, drain cherries, reserving 1/2 cup juice. In a saucepan, combine cherries, reserved cherry juice, brown sugar and granulated sugar; mix well. Bring mixture to a boil over medium heat. Add mustard; mix well. Cook 5 minutes, or until slightly thickened.

After chicken has cooked 30 minutes, remove baking dish from oven. Carefully remove foil cover; spoon hot cherry mixture evenly over chicken. Bake, uncovered, 15 minutes, or until chicken is done. Serve immediately.

Note: 2 cups frozen unsweetened tart cherries can be substituted for canned tart cherries; use 1/2 cup cherry juice blend or water in place of juice from canned cherries.

Makes 6 servings.

Serving size; 2 pieces of a whole chicken or 1 chicken breast half, 224 calories per serving.

Total fat per serving: 4 grams.

CHERRY PINWHEELS

End a special-occasion meal with these delicate, flaky cookies.

1/2 cup 4% fat cream-style cottage cheese (no substitutions)
1 cup all-purpose flour
1 cup butter (no substitutions)
1/2 cup cherry preserves
1 egg white
Granulated sugar

In a large mixing bowl, cottage cheese and flour. Cut in butter. Press dough together and flatten. Divide dough into quarters; wrap in plastic wrap. Refrigerate 4 hours or overnight.

On a well-floured surface, roll out 1 piece of dough in a rectangle about 1/16 inch thick. Dough will be sticky. Keep remaining dough refrigerated. With a sharp knife, cut rectangle into 2 1/2 inch squares. Transfer squares to greased baking sheets. Make 1 inch diagonal cuts from each corner toward the center of each square. Place 1/4 teaspoon jam in the center. Fold every other tip to center over the jam to form a pinwheel. Refrigerate 10 minutes.

Lightly brush tops of dough with egg white; sprinkle with sugar. Bake in a preheated 350 degree oven 12 to 15 minutes, or until golden brown. Let cool.

Makes about 3 dozen.

Serving size: 1 cookie, 76 calories per serving. Total fat per serving: 5 grams.

ROCK CORNISH-SWEET CHERRY FLAMBE

2 Rock Cornish game hens, thawed and halved
Salt and Pepper
Butter or margarine
1 (16-ounce) can dark sweet cherries
2 tablespoons cornstarch
1/2 cup sugar
1 orange, unpeeled, sliced lengthwise
1 teaspoon almond extract
1/2 cup brandy

Put game hens on rack over shallow pan. Salt and pepper, lightly and brush with melted butter. Bake at 350 degrees for about an hour or until done and browned. Drain cherries, reserving syrup. Add water, if needed, to get 1 cup liquid.

Mix cornstarch and sugar in chafing dish or saucepan. Gradually add liquid, stirring constantly until thick and bubbly. Add cherries, orange slices and extract. Heat brandy separately. Pour brandy over sauce in serving dish; ignite.

Appendix A

Microwave Cooking Ideas

With less time to prepare meals, many households are discovering the timesaving joy of microwave cookery. Here are some suggestions to make your microwave cooking experience easier.

• *Do not overcook cherries. As with other fruits, it is best to add them during one of the last cooking steps, if possible.*

• *For even cooking, cut fruit, vegetables and meat into pieces of uniform size and shape. Individual food items, such as potatoes, should be as nearly alike in size and shape as possible.*

• *Read the recipe all the way through, then prepare and measure all the ingredients before you begin cooking. This is particularly important with microwave cookery because once you begin cooking, each step goes quickly.*

• *Follow recipe directions about covering containers. Many recipes require a cover to hold in heat and moisture, which makes the food cook faster and more evenly.*

• *When a recipe says "cover", use a tight-fitting lid or plastic wrap. When using plastic wrap, fold back a corner to create a vent, which helps prevent the wrap from splitting.*

• *Remove covers carefully. Open casseroles and remove plastic wrap by lifting the far corner. This allows steam to escape and helps avoid burns.*

• *Because most recipes require frequent stirring, keep a supply of spoons and a spoon holder near the micro-*

wave. Wooden spoons can be left in the cooking container during the various steps.

• Hot pads often are needed to remove containers of hot food from the microwave. Keep a supply handy.

• More food means more time. If you double the quantity of food, you will need to increase the cooking time by about 60 percent.

• Always choose a container or material that allows microwave energy to pass through it to reach the food. Glass, pottery, china, paper and thermoplastic are the most common materials used in microwave cooking utensils.

• When possible, use containers that are round. Foods cooked in square or rectangular dishes are likely to be overcooked on the corners.

• Never operate your microwave oven unless you have food or liquid in it.

• Be sure to read the manual that came with your oven for specific instructions.

Courtesy of Cherry Marketing Institute

Appendix B

The Cherry Story From The
Cherryland of Northwest Michigan

*Cherries have pleased the palates of food lovers for centuries.
Their ruby-red color and tangy taste won cherries a place on the
tables of Roman conquerors, Greek citizens and Chinese noblemen.*

*European settlers had hardly stepped on the soil of
the New World before they began planting cherry trees. Early
French colonists from Normandy brought pits that they planted
along the Saint Lawrence River and on down into the
Great Lakes area. Cherry trees were part of the gardens of French
settlers as they established such cities as Detroit, Vincennes,
St. Louis and other Midwestern settlements.*

*Peter Dougherty, a Presbyterian missionary, is credited with
planting the first cherry orchard and, in essence, getting the
cherry industry started as a commercial enterprise in the
Grand Traverse Region of Michigan. Against the advice of
local Indian farmers who had grown other fruit trees in the
area, Dougherty planted a cherry orchard in 1852 on the
Old Mission Peninsula. This peninsula is a narrow strip
of land that juts out into Grand Traverse Bay just north
of Traverse City, Michigan. Much to the surprise
of the Indians and others, Dougherty's cherry trees
flourished and soon other residents of the area planted trees.*

*A cherry tree can grow almost anywhere, but commercial
cherry orchards need specific climatic conditions and farming
techniques. Rolling hills and sandy soil are essential for air
flow and water drainage in the orchards. In addition, a large
body of water, such as Lake Michigan, helps to temper the cold
winds and cool the orchards in summer. The Grand Traverse
Region proved to have all of these conditions
for growing cherries commercially.*

The first commercial cherry orchard was planted in 1893 on Ridgewood Farm near the site of Dougherty's original plantings. By the early 1900's the tart cherry industry was firmly established and production surpassed other crops produced in the area. The first cherry processing facility, Traverse City Canning Company, was built just south of Traverse City and cherries soon were shipped out of the region to Chicago, Detroit, Milwaukee and eventually all across the country.

Today there are more than two million cherry trees in the Grand Traverse Region, and Traverse City, in the heart of the region, is called "The Cherry Capital of the World." The Grand Traverse Region, which includes five counties around Traverse City, annually produces about 40 percent of the tart cherries, harvesting about three-forths of the U.S. crops. Commercial orchards dot the state along Lake Michigan from Benton Harbor to the Elk Rapids area. In addition, most of the processing facilities are located near the orchards.

The primary variety of tart cherry grown in the United States today is Montmorency. It has been cultivated in this country for more than a century because the fruit is excellent for pies, preserves, jellies, juices and other products. Horticulturists are experimenting with other tart cherry varieties that may someday have commercial applications.

The amount of tart cherries produced each year varies, depending on a number of factors, including the age of the trees and weather conditions. In 1994, Michigan harvested 210 million pounds of tart cherries; the total tart cherry production for the U.S. was 288 million pounds. In 1993, Michigan harvested 270 million pounds of tart cherries; 215 million pounds in 1992.

Tart cherries, which are sometimes called pie cherries or sour cherries, are seldom sold fresh. They generally are canned or frozen to seal in the fresh taste shortly after harvesting, then are used in many different kind of products throughout the year. Desserts, especially pies, are the most popular products using tart cherries. But consumers can find many other cherry products in local supermarkets including juices, candies, jellies and jams, ice cream and other frozen confections, all kinds of bakery items and specialty products such as mustards and salsa. Dried tart cherries are a relatively new product that are available in some supermarkets and gourmet and specialty stores.

Sweet cherries primarily are grown in the Pacific Coast states, but Michigan joins the top four producers, harvesting about 20 percent of the crop each year, with most of the Michigan production in the Grand Traverse Region. Sweet cherry varieties grown in Michigan include Emperor Francis, Rainier and Schmidt. The Bing variety of sweet cherry is not grown in Michigan; the Schmidt variety, however, is similar to the Bing variety.

Generally, Michigan's sweet cherries are canned, frozen or processed into maraschino cherries. A small percentage of Michigan's sweet cherries are sold fresh, primarily at local farm markets.

Both tart and sweet cherries ripen in July; the third week of July is usually the peak of the harvest. Today almost all of the tart cherries are harvested using a mechanical shaker, which resembles an upside-down umbrella. In early times, most of the cherries were picked by hand, often using migrant harvesters.

In celebration of the fruit that grows so well in the Grand Traverse Region, a spring ceremony known as the "Blessing of the Blossoms" was initiated in 1924. This event eventually became the National Cherry Festival, which is held in Traverse City each year in July. The festival attracts thousands of visitors from all over the world to "cherryland."

Appendix C

*When reducing calories and fat in your recipes,
follow these suggestions:*

• *Season generously with herbs and spices, but reduce
the amount of salt used. Cherries go well with numerous
herbs and spices, including cinnamon, nutmeg, ginger,
mustard, thyme, basil, garlic and dill.*

• *Use low-fat dairy products, but read the labels carefully before purchasing. Some possible substitutions are
skim milk for whole milk; Neufchatel cheese for cream
cheese; and light margarine in place of margarine or butter.*

• *Spray baking pans with a light coating of non-stick
vegetable spray instead of greasing them. Vegetable spray
also can be used when sautéeing or stir-frying foods.*

• *Reduce the amount of sugar used. In most recipes the
amount of sugar generally can be reduced by at least one-
third. It's best not to substitute honey or corn syrup in a
recipe that calls for granulated sugar because honey, corn
syrup and other such sweeteners add liquid to the recipe.
Use recipes especially developed for honey or corn syrup.*

• *Use "lite" versions of products, such as cherry filling
and topping, to reduce calories even further.*

INDEX

ORDERING INFORMATION

Cherry Creations, The Ultimate Cherry Cookbook

If your local bookstore is unable to obtain this book, you may order directly from:

Northstar Publishing
1818 Industrial Dr. Suite 209
Las Vegas, NV 89102
Phone 800-717-6001